Good Wives

A Play in Three Acts

Adapted by
Peter Clapham

From the Novel by
Louisa M. Alcott

A SAMUEL FRENCH ACTING EDITION

New York Hollywood London Toronto
SAMUELFRENCH.COM

Copyright © 1965 by Peter Clapham
All Rights Reserved

GOOD WIVES is fully protected under the copyright laws of the British Commonwealth, including Canada, the United States of America, and all other countries of the Copyright Union. All rights, including professional and amateur stage productions, recitation, lecturing, public reading, motion picture, radio broadcasting, television and the rights of translation into foreign languages are strictly reserved.

ISBN 978-0-573-09332-6

www.samuelfrench.co.uk
www.samuelfrench.com

FOR AMATEUR PRODUCTION ENQUIRIES

UNITED KINGDOM AND WORLD
EXCLUDING NORTH AMERICA
plays@samuelfrench.co.uk
020 7255 4302/01

Each title is subject to availability from Samuel French, depending upon country of performance.

CAUTION: Professional and amateur producers are hereby warned that *GOOD WIVES* is subject to a licensing fee. Publication of this play does not imply availability for performance. Both amateurs and professionals considering a production are strongly advised to apply to the appropriate agent before starting rehearsals, advertising, or booking a theatre. A licensing fee must be paid whether the title is presented for charity or gain and whether or not admission is charged.

The Professional Rights in this play are controlled by Samuel French Ltd, 24-32 Stephenson Way, London NW1 2HD.

No one shall make any changes in this title for the purpose of production. No part of this book may be reproduced, stored in a retrieval system, or transmitted in any form, by any means, now known or yet to be invented, including mechanical, electronic, photocopying, recording, videotaping, or otherwise, without the prior written permission of the publisher. No one shall upload this title, or part of this title, to any social media websites.

The right of Peter Clapham and Louisa M. Alcott to be identified as authors of this work has been asserted in accordance with Section 77 of the Copyright, Designs and Patents Act 1988.

PRODUCTION NOTE

In compiling these notes, I draw on the experience gained during the original production of this play, and hope that they will be a source of help and encouragement to others who may feel tempted to tackle a production of GOOD WIVES, but who hesitate for reasons of restricted stage space or limited finance.

Setting

Admittedly the original production was mounted fairly elaborately—thanks to the generosity of a sympathetic committee, and the good fortune of being able to use a stage of considerable depth on which the setting could be constructed as described—but this setting can be greatly modified for a smaller stage without any marked loss of dramatic effect. The scene is, after all, a simple Colonial parlour and not a vast baronial hall.

The archway at the back with the hall and stairs beyond is an attractive and useful feature as it affords three distinct exits (i.e. upstairs, to the kitchen, and to the front door), but it is by no means vital, and can be dispensed with entirely on a shallow stage where an exit U.C. is difficult to contrive. In this case the exit to the hall should be through an archway in the wall above or below the fireplace R.

The window U.L. can be simplified in a similar way, and could, indeed, be just an ordinary casement window—though a little bow window, if it can be contrived, does give interest and character to the room.

The flats may be painted to resemble Victorian wallpaper of a not too obtrusive pattern, or to give the effect of a dado with wallpaper above it, but all suggestion of "newness" must be avoided. For a description of the general effect at which to aim, one can hardly do better than quote Miss Alcott herself in her earlier book *Little Women*: "It was a comfortable old room, though the carpet was faded and the furniture very plain: for a good picture or two hung on the walls, books filled the recesses, chrysanthemums and Christmas roses bloomed in the windows, and a pleasant atmosphere of home-peace pervaded it."

Furniture

This should present no great problem as Victorian pieces can usually be found fairly easily in most second-hand furniture or even junk shops; and a surprising number of homes possess the odd item or two of Victoriana which can be borrowed as often as not—if the owners are approached in the right way.

I would point out, in passing, that whilst a "worn, faded" look is to be desired, anything which is drab or shabby is to be avoided, for there is a very definite difference. It is the home of a family in reduced circumstances; the furnishings are good and well-cared for, and the whole effect should be clean and bright.

A tremendous sense of period can be achieved by careful attention to detail in such things as ornaments, pictures (*and* their frames), lamps, cushion covers (great opportunity here to achieve both "period" and a splash of colour, for they can be patchwork, bead or woollen embroidered, appliqué work, etc., as well as plain rich colours, preferably in velvet), china, books, cloths, and so on.

The most important items of furniture are, of course, the sofa, the table behind it (the small round ones of the time are ideal as they take up little room and are easy to move around), Marmee's chair by the fire, the cabinet backstage (which can be either the type with glass-fronted bookshelves at the top and cupboards below, or with ordinary cupboard doors both above and below), and, of course, the piano.

The piano used in the original production was a little table-piano of about 1830 which we were fortunate enough to be able to borrow from a local music shop; but an ordinary upright piano, providing it is not too modern in appearance, would do equally well. Whilst on the subject of the piano, it might be encouraging to any actress playing Beth to know that the original could hardly play a note, but by using another piano off-stage and timing it carefully, an effect was produced which deceived, I think, quite ninety per cent of our audiences; at any rate, the actress in question was complimented more than once on her skill as a pianist. This "dubbing" must, however, be carefully rehearsed; we found that by "striking a chord" before starting to "play" the actress was able to follow the ghost-pianist offstage without fear of making a false start.

Costumes

The costumes should be kept fairly simple. Apart from the fact that the family have only limited means, clothes were, at that period, made to last much longer than in the present day, and, as the action of the play covers only a little more than one year, there is no need for numerous changes of costume. Aunt March's clothes should be as rich and elaborate as possible in marked contrast to the rest of the family, and to emphasize her wealth and importance. Aunt Carrol, also, should be well-dressed. Laurie and Mr. Laurence must also give the impression of wealth; variety in the rather sombre and formal male garments of the period can be achieved quite well with a change of waistcoats (about the only concession to colour allowed them) with the same frock-coat and trousers. Professor Bhaer is, of course, a poor man.

Some slight change and variety can be introduced into the ladies' costumes, which will help to underline the passage of time and point any change of season or time of day, by the use of different shawls, collars, fichus, etc. This is especially useful during an Act (where one scene follows swiftly on another), proves most effective, and is easy and quick to contrive.

Careful attention to the matter of hair styles greatly helps a sense of period in any costume play, and GOOD WIVES is no exception. Undoubtedly the side ringlets are very becoming, and it is quite possible that *all* the ladies will feel they ought to have them, but in the case of the four girls, at least, a different hair style should be carefully thought out for each, in keeping with the character, and rigidly adhered to throughout the production.

Lighting

It is not easy to lay down hard and fast rules with regard to a lighting plot as that which will enhance and enrich the colour scheme of one set will prove quite disastrous on another. One can, therefore, only suggest the general effect at which to aim. This should be to create as far as possible—and for the want of a better phraseology—a visual atmosphere of warm, Victorian domesticity. To some that may sound a little vague, but it is something more easily recognized than described, and one which the producer, in conjunction with the electricians, can only achieve by gentle experiment with the set upon which they are working.

In our own case we found that a mixture of orange and white in the lights produced just the right daylight effect, and, for the scenes at night, attractive, and dramatic, pools of light centred on the "oil" lamps (one on either side of the stage) were produced with lavender spots.

It is highly desirable that the lights should be faded in and out on scenes, as described in the script, and every effort should be made to achieve this if it is at all possible. Apart from the fact that it heightens greatly the dramatic effect for the scenes to open and close in this way, it does much to counteract the unavoidably episodic nature of the play and, coupled with the music, helps the whole thing to flow more easily along.

Music

This can be used to very great effect, and its value is twofold. First, it helps in no small measure to create both the right atmosphere and the right period; second, it maintains them and provides continuity during the short black-outs between scenes.

For curtain and continuity music we used "Home, Sweet Home" in a musical-box arrangement which seemed—quite literally—to strike just the right note.

Music should be pre-recorded on tape so that it may be faded gently in and out in conjunction with the lights. This may call for a little time and trouble on someone's part, but its effectiveness should not be under-estimated.

Production

As a period piece, GOOD WIVES calls, of course, for careful attention to such things as movement, the wearing of costume (so that it looks like costume, and not fancy dress) and the manners and speech of a bygone age. Without thought for and preparation in these matters at rehearsal, much is lost in the final production.

The value of low-heeled shoes or dancing pumps (preferably the ones which will actually be worn in performance) and long practice skirts for the ladies, worn from an early stage in rehearsals, cannot be too heavily stressed. This makes for an ease of movement, and lack of consciousness of full skirts in performance which is wholly desirable.

The keynote of the whole production should be simple sincerity, and every effort should be made to create a true "family feeling" among the girls and their mother. This is a difficult, intangible something which cannot be achieved entirely by the dialogue or specific moves; it is something which each member of the family must truly feel and seek ways to express. A look, a smile, a gesture, a touch—these things will suggest themselves to the cast as rehearsals proceed, and the producer should do everything to encourage these refinements of interpretation as well as suggesting his, or her, own. The original cast achieved this sense of warm, family unity to a very fine degree and, thereby, greatly increased the quality of the whole production.

The contrast between the four girls should be brought out to give variety and life, not only to the characters themselves, but to the play as a whole. There can be, of course, no better guide to a complete understanding of each and every part than by a study of the original book. It is more than just a good idea to get the cast to read it during the early stages of rehearsal.

The period and the picturesque costumes lend themselves to attractive grouping, and particular use can be made of this at the opening of nearly all the scenes. A good pace is desirable throughout, and simple, straightforward playing, is all that is required in the more tender scenes. Do *please* avoid all temptation to be over-sentimental or beautifully tragic; it will kill these passages stone dead, and make your audience restless or embarrassed—or both.

I have seen the business of Mr. March closing Beth's piano both movingly done and nauseatingly "hammed".

The opening of each new scene should be lifted and not allowed to drag, so that the audience's interest and attention is immediately recaptured. To this end it is equally important that the black-outs between scenes are kept as short as possible.

It has been stressed already that a feeling of continuity must be maintained, but if the tabs are drawn at the end of each scene the whole quickly develops into an evening of one-act plays. It is necessary, therefore, for members of the cast who are left on the stage at the end of a scene to clear quickly and, above all, quietly during the blackout, and for those who are to open the next scene to take their places with equal speed and silence.

This is quite simple to do, and can be achieved within a remarkably short space of time, but it does require some rehearsal, and for the members of the cast who are to open a scene to be standing by during the previous scene—there is no time for chasing after people who are having a good gossip down in the dressing-rooms.

To prevent wholesale confusion during a change-over it is wise for those concluding a scene to clear first before anyone else sets foot on the stage, and for all backstage personnel to keep well clear during the change. The on-coming cast can be rehearsed in bringing on any new props, and the retiring members in striking anything which would be particularly noticeable (such as somebody's bonnet). This removes the danger of any clash between cast and property people struggling to get things in place.

I feel that there is little to be gained by using an American accent; frequently these can be atrocious, and their very artificiality could prove distracting to an audience. In the original production we played it "straight", and in discussing it afterwards with numerous Alcott devotees I could not find one who thought it in any way amiss for us to do so.

P.C.

N.B. Interleaved producers' copies of this play are available, price 10s. 6d. (postage 7d. extra), *direct from the Publishers only*.

*GOOD WIVES

ACT ONE

Scene 1

The parlour of the MARCH *home is a large, comfortable room. There is a fireplace* D.R.; *at the back a draped archway leads into the hall, in which can be seen the foot of the stairs;* U.L. *is a large bow window beyond which can be glimpsed the shrubs and bushes of a small garden. The room is well and comfortably furnished, but everything is a little worn and faded, for the family who live here are not as prosperous now as they have been. However, this does not make the room any less inviting, for it is always very clean and bright—and made cosy with books, pictures, flowers and potted plants. A pleasant atmosphere of home peace pervades it.*

The play opens early on a fine morning in June in the late 1860s. It is the day of MEG's *wedding and the room has about it a festive air in preparation for this great event. The bow window has been transformed, with garlands and vases of flowers, into a little bower, in which stands a small table covered with a white cloth and on it the family Bible. It is here that the actual ceremony will take place. Around the room are more vases and bowls of flowers.*

The curtain rises in darkness, and the lights come up gently, on MRS. MARCH *and her four daughters.* MEG, *the eldest, in her wedding gown, stands radiant and happy whilst her mother makes a last-minute adjustment with needle and cotton.* BETH *stands besides* MRS. MARCH *looking on approvingly and holding the work-box.* AMY, *seated on a low chair at a little distance, is busy sketching her sister in her simple wedding gown, while* JO, *perched on the back of the sofa, observes the scene with mixed feelings. The romantic flavour of the occasion is not at all to her more practical tastes. However, she cannot but share in her sister's obvious and abundant joy at this time.*

MRS. M. (*finishing off and breaking the thread*). There! It only needed a stitch to catch the seam down. (*Straightening up with a look of affectionate approval.*) Well, Meg, my dear, you have put a great deal of loving care into making your wedding gown, and I declare it shows in every stitch. John will fall in love with you all over again when he sees you in it, I am sure.

BETH. Oh, Meg, you look so very sweet and lovely that I could hug you, but I'm afraid I should crumple your dress.

MEG (*with a smile of deep contentment*). Then I am satisfied. But please hug and kiss me, everyone, and don't mind my dress; I want a great many crumples of that sort put into it today. (*She embraces* MRS. MARCH *and* BETH.)

AMY (*critically, but not unkindly—she is ever a devotee of the fashion plates*).

*It is illegal to perform this play, in any circumstances whatsoever, without a licence. Please refer, for full details, to Copyright Notice preceding main text. (Copyright Act 1956.)

Yes, it is certainly very becoming, and you have worked long and patiently at it; but I do think that, for a wedding gown, you could have made it a little more stylish. It is too simple for the present vogue—you need more lace and ribbon trimming, and I think that orange blossom at the throat and waist would have looked sweetly pretty.

MEG (*moving to her with an affectionate smile and hug*). Now, Amy, dear, you know that I said from the first that I wanted a simple, homely wedding. I have no desire for it to be a grand, fashionable affair, or for me to look like a fine lady in a fashion plate. I want only those about me whom I love, and for them I wish to look, and be, my familiar self. (*She kisses* AMY.) As for orange blossom, I will neither wear nor carry any flowers but lilies of the valley, for they are John's favourite. (*Turning to* Jo.) Well, Jo? Why so glum? This is my wedding day, you know, and I want everyone to be happy with me. Don't say that you are still vexed with John for taking me away from you all, as you put it! It is three years now since we became engaged and I thought that you had got used to the idea. Anyway, we are to live only such a very short distance from here that I shall be as much part of the family as ever!

Jo (*with a little sigh*). You will never be that again, Meg. I know at first I did rather resent John coming and, as it seemed to me, breaking up our little family circle, but I have grown more sensible in the last three years, and I realize now that we were bound to lose you sooner or later. You are much too pretty to be left for long before some fine gentleman came to carry you off—and I would rather it was John Brooke than anyone else I know. (*She embraces* MEG.)

MEG. Thank you, Jo, for saying that. But I don't want any of you to feel that I am separated from you, or that I love you any the less for loving John so much. I shall come to see you every single day and expect to keep my old place in your hearts, though I am married. (*Moving to the window.*) You can see our little home-to-be among the trees along the road, and you must drop in whenever you can to laugh at my housekeeping struggles.

AMY (*as she packs her drawing things away*). If you only had a servant or two you wouldn't have to struggle.

BETH. Mrs. Hummel's eldest girl, Lotty, is going to come in every day to run errands and help here and there. That will make things easier for Meg, and leave her just enough work to keep her from getting homesick!

AMY. Sallie Moffat has four servants in her new home.

Jo. If Meg had four in hers the house wouldn't hold them, and master and missus would have to camp out in the garden.

MRS. M. One should not make comparisons, Amy. Ned Moffat is a very rich young man, and Sallie is fortunate in marrying someone who can give her a fine house, a carriage, and everything else she wants. Meg and John begin humbly, but I have a feeling that there will be quite as much happiness in their little house as in the Moffats' big one. (*Turning to* MEG.) One thing troubles me, though; Sallie is your friend, you have grown up together and you are now marrying within a very short time of each other. It is only natural that you should be aware of the difference in your circumstances, and for you to contrast their fine establishment with your own more modest little house. I hope, my dear, that you do not feel dissatisfied with it in any way—and that you believe that you will be happy there?

MEG (*moving to her mother*). Oh, Mother, I am perfectly satisfied—thanks to everyone's efforts to make me feel so—and so happy that I can't talk about it.

MRS. M. Then I am happy, too. (*Turning to include them all.*) My heart is full of gratitude, for I feel I have so much to be thankful for just now—that dreadful war over at last; your father home again safe and sound, and busy in his parish once more; and, then, this very special happiness today. (*Looking at the clock and adopting a brisker tone.*) But, goodness me, we mustn't waste time like this! There are still a few things left to do, and it will not be long before our guests start to arrive.

AMY. The dining-room is all laid out and decorated, Marmee; we have only to arrange things in here and we shall be quite ready.

BETH. Your little wedding bower looks really elegant, Amy.

JO. Yes, it makes a perfect setting for the family nuptials! Now, if we put the sofa over there in front of the fireplace it will do nicely for Aunt March—she'll be able to see and hear everything in comfort without being in the way. Come on, Amy, give me a hand. We shall have a long face and raised eyebrows if Aunt March doesn't have the place of honour.

(*They move the sofa and set it in place.*)

That's better. I wonder what's happened to that high-spirited young neighbour of ours, Laurie? He said he'd be over early to see if there was anything he could do to help.

AMY. What a thing it is to have a harum-scarum college boy in and out of the house all the time.

JO. You know you love it, and you like it even better when he brings his harum-scarum college companions with him. You are quite a belle among them—and well you know it!

AMY (*slightly affronted by this accusation—although she knows it to be true*). I am sure I only try to be a gracious hostess. Whether I become a great artist or not, I am resolved to grow to be an attractive and accomplished woman, and it is good practice for me to help entertain Laurie's friends.

JO. Well, he hasn't brought any with him this week because of Meg's wedding, so you will have to make do with being gracious to Aunt March when she arrives, and, goodness knows, you need to be attractive and accomplished to do that!

BETH. Now he is at college we don't see nearly as much of Laurie as we used to in the old days.

MRS. M. It's difficult to remember how shy he was when he and his grandfather first moved into the big house next door; but once Jo had taken him in hand he practically lived here! Not that I minded for a moment—he has made up for the brother you never had, and I think we helped a lonely boy who had only an old man for company.

MEG. If Laurie and his grandfather had not moved next door, a certain Mr. John Brooke would never have come to be Laurie's tutor and none of what is happening today would have come to pass; for that reason alone, Laurie has a very warm place in my heart!

JO (*who has moved to the window*). Well, speak of angels and they flap their wings. Here he comes now, and with what looks like yet another of his special wedding presents for you, Meg.

MEG. Oh, no! I wish he wouldn't waste his money so; every week he comes home with some fresh absurdity. What can it be this time?

JO. It looks pretty fearsome, but nothing could be worse than that sweeper he brought last week which neatly took the nap off the carpet and left the dirt behind!

(*The front-door bell is heard to ring and the front door opens.* LAURIE'S *voice is heard calling and in reply to it there is a chorus of* "Come in, Laurie!" *from the girls. A moment later* LAURIE *appears in the archway; he is resplendent in his wedding attire, which includes a very dashing new waistcoat and a colourful buttonhole. He is carrying a gaily wrapped parcel of curious shape.*)

LAURIE (*with a gallant flourish*). The best man presents himself! Greetings to you ladies all—and special felicitations to you, ma'am, on your wedding morn. (*He makes an elaborate mock bow to* MEG.)

MRS. M. Thank you, Laurie. How is our boy today?

LAURIE (*kissing* MRS. MARCH). Ready for anything on this festive occasion!

JO. Which side won the match yesterday, Laurie?

LAURIE. Ours, of course! Wish you'd been there to see. Amy, you are getting altogether too handsome for a single lady.

AMY. And how is the lovely Miss Randal?

LAURIE (*affecting a broken heart*). More cruel than ever; don't you see how I am pining away? (*Presenting the parcel to* MEG.) For Mrs. John Brooke with the maker's congratulations and compliments!

MEG. Thank you, Laurie, but where is John? I thought he would come with you.

LAURIE. He told me to come on ahead and to say that he wouldn't be long. It seems that all his fingers have turned to thumbs in the night and, as a result, he is having some slight difficulty in tying his cravat to his complete satisfaction.

BETH. What's your latest wonderful discovery for Meg's new home? Undo the parcel and let us see, please!

LAURIE (*affecting offended dignity*). You must promise not to laugh at it; you have been very cruel about some of my labour-saving devices.
JO. Well, when they are like that famous nutmeg-grater of yours which fell to pieces at the first trial, you can hardly blame us!
LAURIE (*unpacking the parcel, as the others laugh, and speaking in the manner of a fair-ground barker*). Have you ever thought, ma'am, what you would do if your husband was away from home, and the house broken into by thieves, footpads, cut-throats or murderers? What would you do if the little homestead was overcome by fire, flood, famine, or fatal pestilence? All you would have to do in your hour of dire necessity would be to open your front window, and with this ingenious contrivance, but newly invented, rouse the entire neighbourhood in a jiffy!

(*From the wrappings he whisks out a watchman's rattle, and immediately demonstrates its powers—accompanying the performance with loud shouts of* "Help! Help! Fire! Murder!" *etc. Recovering from the initial shock, the girls fall on him with laughter and cries of remonstrance in an attempt to bring an end to the uproar. The battle is still in progress, when* HANNAH *appears suddenly from the kitchen—more than a little alarmed by the noise.*)
HANNAH. Land sakes! What's to do? I thought the Angels of the Lord were descending in judgment! (*Seeing* LAURIE.) Oh, it's you, Mister Laurie! I might have known; you're that full of life you very near scare it out of other folks.
MRS. M. I am sorry if you were alarmed, Hannah, but I assure you it was as unexpected for us as it must have been for you! Laurie, come and say that you're sorry.
LAURIE. Forgive me, Hannah. I promise never ever to do it again as long as we both shall live, amen.
HANNAH. I should hope not, indeed. I was just putting the cake on the stand, mum, and I all but dropped it.
JO. Oh, the wedding cake! Laurie, you must come and see the wedding cake. Marmee and Hannah have made a real plummy one, haven't they, girls?
AMY.
BETH. } Oh, yes, it's a beauty!

(*They seize him by the hand and make for the kitchen.*)
HANNAH (*to* JO *and the others as they depart*). Mind now—no picking!
MEG. I'm afraid that the preparations for today have meant a lot of extra work for you, Hannah. I hope it hasn't been too much for you.
HANNAH (*her tone immediately softer; taking* MEG *by the hand*). Bless you, Miss Meg, it's all been a labour o' love for me and your ma. I've seen you grow from a babby to a fine young woman, and I should like to know who else but me should help to prepare your marriage feast! Everything's laid out a treat in the dining-room, and Miss Amy's made the table that pretty with her "flowery arrangements"

as she calls them. She's the artistic one and no mistake. A real banquet it looks. I've only the cake to titivate now, and then I can get myself ready for the cerrymoany.

MRS. M. What are you going to wear, Hannah?

HANNAH. Ah! My new shawl, o' course, and then I've made myself a very special kind of hat for the occasion.

MEG. A new hat?

HANNAH. Well, not quite a hat. I copied it from a picture in one of those fashion journals Miss Amy's always reading. It was called "a stylish headdress for the opera or any special occasion". Well, I'm never likely to see no opera, but if Miss Meg's wedding ain't "a special occasion"—I'd like to know what is!

MRS. M. It certainly is, and we shall look forward to seeing this "stylish headdress"!

HANNAH. It took me a tidy time to make, and I didn't want no one to see it before it was finished. Mister Laurie and the girls are very quiet; I'm always mistrustful when they're like that! I'll away to my kitchen, I think, before that young whirlwind sits on the cake—or worse!

(*She goes out anxiously as* MR. MARCH *is seen descending the stairs. A smile of affectionate amusement for* HANNAH *passes between* MRS. MARCH *and* MEG. MR. MARCH *enters the parlour.*)

MR. M. (*with a smile*). Judging by the sounds of hilarious uproar which penetrated to my study I gather that our boisterous young neighbour has descended upon us once again! At any rate, I thought it was time for me to lay aside Sunday's sermon and turn my attention to the festivities of the day.

(*There is the sound of laughter and voices from the direction of the kitchen, above which rises a wail from* HANNAH—"Now then Mister Laurie, put it down this instant before you drop it!")

Presumably the young man has now turned his attention to the kitchen?

MEG. Yes, Father; the girls wanted to show him the cake, but I am not at all sure that it was quite the wisest thing to do.

MR. M. Oh, I don't doubt that Hannah will defend her domain to the death—and banish Master Laurie if she thinks it necessary. (*Putting an arm round* MEG.) So you are to be the first bride, eh, Meg? Bless me, it seems but a short time ago that I used to call you my "little women", and now— Well, Margaret, I suppose it may not be so very long before the others will follow her good example?

MRS. M. Oh, I am not so sure, Arthur. Jo has several admirers, but she will do nothing to encourage them. She says that she has no time for "philandering", as she calls it, and wishes only to devote herself to her writing.

MR. M. She is certainly a dedicated soul when it comes to literature. I am glad that she is now getting her short stories accepted regularly, and I hope that all the work she is putting into her novel will bring a just reward; but I should like to see her happy, also, with the man of her choice. I try not to be too inquisitive about my family's personal affairs, but it has seemed to me that, of late, our Laurie has been getting fonder than ever of Jo. Would you agree with me?

MEG. I don't think there is any doubt about it, Father. But she is so brusque with the poor boy whenever he pays her a compliment or tries to show his feelings, that I wonder he has not lost heart; and if ever we raise the subject or try to joke her about it she scolds us so that we think it better to say nothing.

MR. M. Well, well, it may only be a passing phase with her; perhaps time will change things. And what of Beth? She is eighteen now, is she not?

MRS. M. Yes, how fast they do grow up! But Beth, I fear, is as shy as ever with strangers. You know, Arthur, I get anxious about her at times. She has never been quite her old self since she was so very ill with scarlet fever three years ago.

MR. M. But, my dear, she has seemed unusually well lately—busying herself with the rest of you in the wedding arrangements and in setting Meg's new home to rights. What makes you think that something is amiss?

MRS. M. It is not her health that troubles me; it is her spirits. At times she seems unaccountably sad, and now and then I see a look in her face that I don't understand. It isn't like Beth and it worries me.

MEG. I think she is just growing up, Mother, and so begins to dream dreams, and have hopes, and fears, and fidgets, without knowing why or being able to explain them.

MRS. M. Yes, you are probably right. Well, Arthur, that only leaves Amy, and I think she is a little young yet to think of following Meg's example! Anyway, she seems to be too absorbed in her artistic endeavours, and determination to grow into an elegant, accomplished young lady.

MR. M. I have noticed that she is not so occupied with those pursuits to neglect Laurie's college friends when he brings them to call. She positively holds court in here—and I am not at all sure that she hasn't broken a few hearts already.

MRS. M. Now, Mr. March, you are being a regular old gossip, and we have no time for such things on a busy day like this! (*Taking his arm.*) Come, or we shall not be ready to receive our guests.

MR. M. (*with good-humoured resignation*). Very well, my dear. (*To* MEG *as he goes.*) When John arrives I should like to see you both in the study for a little time together before the ceremony, Meg.

MEG (*kissing him*). Yes, Father, of course.

    (MR. *and* MRS. MARCH *go upstairs.* MEG *proceeds to put various little final touches to the room as* JO *and* LAURIE *reappear from the kitchen.*)

Jo (*as she enters*). Oh, Meg, do go to the kitchen! Hannah and Amy cannot decide between them on the final decoration for the cake. One wants a white satin ribbon and the other a garland of flowers. I can't see that it matters very much either way for it'll be eaten up soon enough. (Meg *moves up and goes out to the kitchen during this speech.*) It was all I could do to keep Laurie from picking at it as it was and— (*She turns to discover* Laurie *surreptitiously eating icing sugar behind her back.*) Oh, you wretched, thieving boy! (*She pushes him down on to the sofa and stands over him.*) Will you ever grow up?

Laurie. I'm doing my best, ma'am, but I'm afraid six feet is about all men can do in these degenerate days.

Jo. Now, Laurie, I want to talk seriously to you about today. You must promise to behave well, and not get up to any pranks and spoil the arrangements.

Laurie (*with mock sobriety*). No pranks.

Jo. And don't say funny things when we ought to be sober.

Laurie. I never do! *You* are the one for that.

Jo. And I implore you not to look at me during the ceremony, for I shall certainly laugh if you do.

Laurie. You won't see me; you'll be crying so hard that the thick fog around you will obscure the prospect.

Jo. I never cry unless it is for some great affliction.

Laurie. Such as when I went off to college for the first time, hey?

Jo. Don't be a peacock! I only moaned a trifle to keep the girls company.

Laurie. Well, please don't lecture me any more, there's a good soul. I have enough all the week, and like to enjoy myself when I come home. (*Displaying the colourful garment.*) You haven't remarked upon my new waistcoat. I got it especially for the occasion.

Jo. But you already have seventeen! I thought you'd got over the dandy period, but every now and then it seems to break out in a new spot.

Laurie. Jo, I said "don't lecture any more". By the way, my roommate, Parker, is getting really desperate about Amy. He talks of her constantly, writes poetry, and moons about in a most suspicious manner. I suppose you will say that he had better get rid of these romantic notions, hey?

Jo. He most certainly had! Mercy on us, we don't want any more marrying in this family for years to come!

Laurie. It's a fast age, ma'am, and I don't know what we are coming to. You are a mere infant, but you'll go next, Jo, and we'll be left lamenting.

Jo. Me! Don't be alarmed; I'm not one of the agreeable sort. Nobody will want me, and it's a mercy, for there should always be one old maid in a family.

Laurie (*suddenly serious*). You won't give anyone a chance, Jo. If a fellow tries to show that he likes you, you get so thorny that he doesn't dare go near you.

Jo. I don't like that sort of thing; I'm too busy to be worried with nonsense, and I think it's dreadful to break up families so. Oh, Christmas! Meg's wedding has turned all our heads, and we talk of nothing but lovers and—and—and such absurdities. I don't wish to get raspy, so let's change the subject.

LAURIE. Mark my words, Jo, you'll go next.

(*Before she can find a suitable retort,* MEG, BETH *and* AMY *reappear from the kitchen. There has obviously been a clash of opinion on the important matter of decorating the cake.*)

AMY (*decidedly*). I still think that it would look better with just the flowers.

BETH (*anxious to avoid any unpleasantness*). Never mind, Amy, it looks delightful as it is; now, we really must go up and change. (*She takes* AMY *by the arm and they go upstairs.*)

MEG (*re-entering the parlour*). Well, I've settled the matter by having the satin ribbon *and* the garland of flowers—so both Hannah and Amy are happy now. (*With an anxious look upstairs after the retreating figure of* AMY.) At least, I hope so.

Jo (*moving to* MEG). I've given Laurie a good talking to, and he's promised to— (*The front-door bell interrupts her.*) Oh, Christmas! I hope that's not Aunt March already! (*She goes out to the front door.*)

MEG. Now, you know what to do, don't you, Laurie? You stand over here (*She indicates a position* L. *of the window.*)—by John, and then at luncheon you will make a little speech, won't you, just to— (*She breaks off as* JO *re-enters dramatically.*)

Jo. Here's the blushing bridegroom!

(JOHN BROOKE *enters, his normal, quiet composure slightly upset by the excitement of the day. He comes into the room a little way and stops short on seeing* MEG. *For a moment they stand quietly looking at one another; then, for once,* JO *rises to the occasion; with waves and signals she tries to indicate to* LAURIE *that it would be tactful to withdraw.* LAURIE, *however, is too preoccupied in watching the others with detached amusement. After one or two more unsuccessful gesticulations,* JO, *with a muttered "*Oh, bother the boy!*" marches forward, seizes him by the nearest ear, and leads him off to the kitchen.*)

LAURIE. Oh, here, I say! Easy on, Jo! What's the idea? Look out, you're hurting!

JOHN (*without moving*). Hello, Meg.

MEG (*also without moving*). Hello, John. (*She suddenly becomes aware of the pinafore she is wearing, and starts to fumble with it.*) Oh dear, I've still got this on—I meant to be all ready when you came and to be really— (*Her words trail away as* JOHN *steps forward swiftly and, taking her in his arms, kisses her tenderly.*)

Oh, John, John!

JOHN. My dearest; how are you?

MEG. Happy, my dear, oh, so very happy! How did you get on with your cravat? Laurie said you were having trouble.

JOHN. I've done the best I can with it. How does it look?

MEG (*adjusting the neckwear with wifely care*). Very elegant! Look! How do you like the way we have set everything out? Amy has made this pretty bower where Father will conduct the ceremony; you will stand here with Laurie beside you; Beth at the piano, of course; and then over here (*Indicating sofa.*)—we have made a place of honour for Aunt March, who would be—

JOHN. So Aunt March has finally condescended to come?

MEG. Yes, John. She's not really such a cross-patch as she likes to make out, you know.

JOHN. She was certainly very unpleasant when we were first engaged. I didn't mind her disapproval of me—"a penniless tutor", I think she called me—

MEG. Oh, John!

JOHN. Well, it was true at the time; but she needn't have been so unkind to you.

MEG. But she repented of it—she's just quick-tempered that's all—and proud, oh, so proud! You know that she said she would have nothing more to do with us if we married—and that all she should give me would be the pearls of Grandmama's, which were long promised to the first bride?

JOHN. And isn't that all she has given you?

MEG. No. You see, she regretted her hastiness, but was too proud to go back on what she had said: so she persuaded Aunt Carrol to buy and send all that lovely house and table linen—and to pretend that it was from her and not Aunt March. Aunt Carrol did as she was asked, but couldn't bear the deception, so she confided the truth to Mother last night. How we laughed when we heard!

JOHN. The wily old thing! Well, I promise to be extra nice to her today by way of return.

MEG. Oh, but you mustn't mention the linen or poor Aunt Carrol will be in terrible trouble.

JOHN. Very well, I promise! Now, who else will be here?

MEG. Well, Aunt Carrol is coming, but she will be alone, as Uncle Carrol has a chill, and Cousin Florence is away at school. So, you see, it will be just the family—and, of course, old Mr. Laurence, who is as much one of us now, as he has been a father to you. Then the Moffats and the Gardiners are coming in later to drink our health.

JOHN (*taking* MEG *in his arms once more*). How does it feel to be marrying a poor orphan without kith or kin?

MEG. No different from how it would feel if you had a score of brothers and sisters, and a whole army of aunts! How could that make any difference? (*She kisses him again.*) Now, Father wants to see us in his study; but before we go up, John, would you refasten this garland, please? It must have slipped down after Amy had finished the bower; she will be so vexed if it isn't all perfect, and it won't take a moment.

JOHN. It needs a little tack just here.

MEG. Amy left the hammer and tacks in the hall. I'll get them. (*She goes off.*)

JOHN (*admiring the bower*). Amy has surpassed herself, hasn't she?

MEG (*off*). You wait until you see the dining-room! (*As she reappears the front-door bell rings loudly.*) I'll just see who that is. (*Taking the hammer and tacks with her she goes off.*)

    (*A moment later* AUNT MARCH *appears in the doorway. She is followed by* AUNT CARROL. AUNT MARCH *is well into the room before she notices* JOHN, *on a chair, examining the garland.*)

AUNT M. (*as she enters*). Mercy on us! I've never heard of such a thing! Answering the door in your wedding gown and an apron! What's happened to that Hannah-woman of yours? Isn't she supposed— (*She suddenly catches sight of* JOHN.) What's all this, then? I have no idea what you are about, Mr. Hook, but it seems to me to be highly improper employment for a bridegroom on his wedding morning!

MEG (*moving into the parlour, and indicating the sofa*). Do sit down and be comfortable, Aunt March, Aunt Carrol. (AUNT CARROL *accepts this invitation gracefully, but* AUNT MARCH *is immovable.*) John and I are just making some finishing touches; we shall not be but a moment or two, and then I'll go up and tell Mother that you have arrived.

AUNT M. Well, upon my word, here's a state of things! Mr. Rook climbing over the furniture like a mountain goat, and you, Meg, waltzing about in your wedding gown for all to see. Don't you know, child, that you oughtn't to appear until the very last minute?

MEG. Now, Aunty, I'm not a show, and no one is coming to stare at me, to criticize my dress, or count the cost of my luncheon. I'm too happy to care what anyone says or thinks, and I'm going to have my little wedding just as I like it. John, dear, here is your hammer.

    (*Taking it with a smile,* JOHN *bends down and kisses her.* AUNT MARCH *is outraged.*)

AUNT M. Mercy on us! I've never heard of such goings on! All I can say—

    (*There is a loud crash and scream from the kitchen.*)

LAURIE (*off* R.). Jupiter Ammon! Jo's dropped the cake!

AUNT M. Dear Heaven! What next!

    (JO *appears carrying a large single-tier wedding cake.* LAURIE *is close behind, laughing heartily.*)

JO. It's all right, Meg, don't take any notice. It's only Laurie up to his pranks—although he promised to behave. Hello, Aunt March! Hello, Aunt Carrol! (*To* LAURIE.) Go on, you mischief-maker, and open the dining-room door for me. (LAURIE *complies and they go off.*)

AUNT M. Upon my word! Josephine and that rattle-pated boy do not improve with the passing years!

MEG. Oh, they mean no harm, Aunt March; it is just high spirits. How is Uncle, Aunt Carrol? I am sorry he won't be with us today.

AUNT C. He is better, thank you, my dear; it is only a slight chill, but, as we are due to go abroad next month, he does not wish to take any risks, and is keeping to his room until he is quite well again. He sends his warmest felicitations, and hopes that he may call to see you in your new home before we leave.

MEG. But, of course, I shall be delighted to receive you both. You are going to Europe, are you not?

AUNT C. Yes; now that Florence is finishing at school—she returns home next week—we thought that a trip to Europe would help to complete her education.

MEG. How she must be looking forward to it! Jo and Amy will envy her, I know, for they both have a great ambition to travel; Jo wants to find new inspiration for her writing, and Amy longs to see all the art treasures about which she has read. (AUNT MARCH *and* AUNT CARROL *exchange a quick glance.*)

AUNT M. Well, Meg, and is your little pill-box of a house all ready for you to move in?

MEG. Oh, yes, quite ready! Everyone has been wonderfully kind and generous to us—

JOHN. Yes, indeed, we have had some handsome presents (*To* AUNT MARCH.)—and, perhaps, this might be a good opportunity for us to thank you for yours, ma'am.

AUNT M. I cannot see that a string of pearls will afford you much comfort, Mr. Book.

JOHN (*pleasantly*). Ah, but there was something more, was there not? The thought which prompted the gift—that is what counts!

MEG (*rising, uncertain of what may follow*). Er—John—I—er—think Father will be waiting for us. (*She seizes* JOHN's *arm and turns to go.*) Will you excuse us, please? Mother will be down directly.

AUNT M. You have a treasure there, Mr. Cook; see that you deserve it!

JOHN. I will do my best, ma'am. Forgive me, but I have noticed that, although our acquaintance is now of some three years' standing, you still experience difficulty in memorizing my surname. It occurs to me that, as I am shortly to become a member of the family circle, your problem might be resolved quite simply if, henceforth, you call me by my Christian name, which is John—whilst, in return, I will have pleasure in calling you Aunt March. Come Meg. (*Quietly triumphant, he goes out, with* MEG *on his arm.*)

AUNT M. Well, upon my word! What are young people coming to? Things are very different from my young days. I would never have dared to speak to my elders like that, I can assure you.

AUNT C. Now, my dear, you mustn't be vexed just because John had the better of you there—after all, you did rather provoke him.

AUNT M. Not at all! He is headstrong! Well, he's marrying into a headstrong family, so they are well matched. But what can one expect? Those girls were allowed far too much freedom when they were younger. Their father would go off to the war as a chaplain; I couldn't for the life of me see why, and I said as much.

AUNT C. (*who has heard the story before*). Yes, of course, the war must be blamed for many things; but I am sure Arthur did only what he thought right.

AUNT M. That's as may be, but the family are the poorer as a result. He is headstrong, too—always helping lame dogs over stiles, though, goodness knows, he can ill afford such luxuries.

AUNT C. I rather think that he sees them as the duties of a practising Christian. He is much loved in his parish, is he not?

(AUNT MARCH *grunts in unwilling agreement.*)

Then I am sure that neither his family nor his parishioners would have him change his ways.

(MR. LAURENCE *appears in the archway, followed by* JO *and* LAURIE.)

Why, here is our last guest! Good morning, Mr. Laurence. We have been looking forward to seeing you again. How are you?

MR. L. My dear ladies! What a pleasure this is! I hope I find you well?

AUNT M. It may interest you to know, Mr. Laurence, that I lay the full blame for today's events at your door.

MR. L. Indeed, ma'am, I—I fear that I don't quite follow—

AUNT M. Oh, come, sir! Don't be so slow-witted. If you had not engaged this John Brooke as a tutor for your harum-scarum grandson here, he would never have set eyes on my niece.

MR. L. I am sure, dear lady, that you could not wish for a finer, more upright young man—

AUNT M. Oh, yes, yes! Maybe, maybe. He's well enough, I know, but I had set my heart on that girl making a rich marriage, and I don't like being thwarted. You could hardly term this a wealthy alliance, now could you?

MR. L. There are different forms of wealth, ma'am, and I do not think that Meg will be the poorer by this marriage. Brooke has good sense and sturdy independence. I offered to do what I could to help him start in business on his own if he so wished; but he preferred to start at the bottom as an under-bookkeeper and make his own way up. For that I admire him, and I believe he will do well.

AUNT M. Humph! My niece married to an under-bookkeeper! A pretty state of affairs, I must say!

JO. Oh, really, Aunt March! How can you! He has more than proved his worth! When Laurie went off to college John could easily have taken another position as a tutor; but, instead, he went off to the war and did his duty manfully until he was wounded and sent home. He didn't get any medals, but he certainly deserved them, for he cheerfully risked all he had. Now he has started in business and is not ashamed to begin at the bottom. He is independent and does not wish to feel under an obligation to anyone; I can understand, for that is my own disposition. With Meg's help I am sure he will get on—and I, for one, am glad that she is marrying him!

AUNT M. Highty-tighty then, miss! You are very free with your opinions, I must say!

(MRS. MARCH *and* BETH *enter. During the ensuing dialogue* MR. MARCH *and* JOHN BROOKE *join the others;* JO *goes upstairs; and* BETH *crosses to the piano, which she starts to play softly.*)

MRS. M. Aunt March! Aunt Carrol! And Mr. Laurence! What must you think of me, not being here to receive you? The house has been in such a turmoil since first thing this morning that we have hardly known whether we were coming or going! Jo, dear, Meg wants you—will you go up? How are you, Aunt March? Is your leg troubling you again? Aunt Carrol—is Uncle a little better today?

(*A moment's general conversation ensues, until* HANNAH *suddenly appears in her wedding attire, greatly excited.*)

HANNAH. The cake's all right, mum, despite that Mister Laurie's pranks, and everything looks lovely!

BETH, *who has been watching the stairs, suddenly breaks into the Bridal March from "Lohengrin". This is a signal for everyone to take up their positions for the ceremony. A silence falls as* MEG, *veiled and carrying her little posy of lilies of the valley, followed by* JO *and* AMY, *begins slowly to descend. In the archway she pauses for a moment and impulsively embraces her mother.* MRS. MARCH, *taking* MEG'S *hand, leads her gently forward to* JOHN BROOKE, *who has turned slightly and is holding out his hand.* MEG, *with a slight shyness, offers hers, and he clasps it gently but firmly in his; together they turn to face* MR. MARCH *who begins to read the opening words of the Marriage Ceremony. For a moment there is no other sound, then a slight rustle breaks the silence; it is* AUNT MARCH *as she surreptitiously pulls out a pocket handkerchief and puts it to her eyes, then suddenly sniffs audibly. As the ceremony proceeds the lights gradually fade.*

SCENE 2

Later that day. As the lights come up we find the parlour much as we left it, but without occupants. From the direction of the front door comes the sound of laughter and cheering; voices are heard calling "Goodbye", "Good luck", etc., as the bridal couple depart on their honeymoon. After a moment or two the noise subsides, and AUNT MARCH *and* AUNT CARROL *appear in the archway.*

AUNT M. Mercy on us; what a fuss and to-do-ment! A body would think they were off to China for their honeymoon instead of just a few hundred yards down the road to that little brown house of theirs. "Dovecote", they call it. Humph! Well, we shall see how long the billing and cooing lasts!

AUNT C. Now, now, my dear, it's no use pretending that you don't wish them well, or, for that matter, that you haven't been moved by their charming little wedding. Your handkerchief was quite sodden before the ceremony was half over.

AUNT M. Really, Mary, you must be getting old and simple. You know perfectly well that I have a slight affliction of the eyes. They are always inclined to water if I am long in an airless room like this—and, anyway, what can you expect with all this garden produce festooned about the place like a harvest thanksgiving? All that pollen being discharged into the atmosphere—most unhealthy! Now, whilst we have a few minutes alone, let us continue the discussion we were having in the carriage on our way here. You say that you would have no objection to taking one of the girls to Europe with you?

AUNT C. None at all, providing that their mother and father will consent. It would be very agreeable for Florence to have some young company whilst we are abroad. They could go off together to visit all the showplaces and beauty-spots. I fear I shall find the "getting about" somewhat tiring; however, Florence is inexhaustible, and it would be nice for her to have a girl of about her own age with whom she could share her excursions. But are you sure you would want to pay for such an expedition without their knowing about it? Wouldn't it be better if you said—

AUNT M. Quite sure, Mary, so there is no point in discussing the matter. I will supply the money, but I prefer that they know nothing about it. The question is—who shall it be? Meg, of course, cannot be considered now, and Beth is, I fear, too delicate to undertake a lot of travelling. (*Almost to herself.*) She is not well, that child.

AUNT C. Besides, she is shy, and I do not think that the prospect would appeal to her greatly. Beth is a little home-bird.

AUNT M. Well, that leaves Josephine and Amy—and there, I fancy, one would be as keen as the other to go.

AUNT C. You have had both as companion at different times, have you not? Which would you suggest?

AUNT M. That is not an easy question to answer, for they each have different qualities—and faults. Josephine was with me for about a year or so after she left school. But when she had to stay at home to help nurse Beth during that nasty attack of scarlet fever I had Amy in her place. Josephine suited me very well, and she can read aloud with good dramatic effect—though she made it clear that she didn't care for my choice of books.

AUNT C. And what of Amy?

AUNT M. She is always very willing and helpful—and, to my mind, improves with each day that passes. Mind you, after she came to me I arranged for her to have drawing lessons—she has an obvious talent—and that so captivated her that she cannot do enough to pleasure me in return.

AUNT C. Indeed, it is a problem. Jo would be a lively companion, and, as the elder of the two, should, perhaps, be given preference; but Amy has the greater flair for social life, the ability to make herself agreeable in company—

AUNT M. Let them settle it for themselves, Mary! They will be coming in directly and I think one or two carefully worded questions will decide the matter without their being any the wiser.

AUNT C. Yes, that would be a possible solution—

AUNT M. It's the obvious solution. Ssh! Someone's coming! I fancy that it will not take us long to make up our minds!

(AMY and BETH *appear in the archway, talking excitedly; they are followed by* HANNAH *and* JO, *who are also in conversation.* JO *takes* AMY'S *arm and leads her into the parlour, whilst* BETH *and* HANNAH *go out to the kitchen.*)

JO (*as she enters*). Come on, Amy, we'd better make the parlour tidy once again. (*To* AUNT MARCH *and* AUNT CARROL.) Mother and Father are walking over to the big house with Mr. Laurence and Laurie, Aunts; they won't be long.

AMY. They said they hoped that you would excuse them for a few minutes, and that you would be able to stay and take tea with us.

AUNT C. Thank you, Amy dear, but Aunt March and I are due at Mrs. Chester's for tea. We must go, for she wishes to discuss the arrangement for her charity fair next week.

AUNT M. Are you girls going to help with it?

AMY. Yes, I have said I will; Mrs. Chester asked me if I would like to help, and I have offered to take charge of a table if she wishes it.

JO. Well, I'm not! Excuse me, Aunt March, but we must put this back into its right place. Catch hold of the other end, Amy!

AUNT M. Well, really! Upon my word! (*She rises indignantly.*)

JO (*unperturbed, as she and* AMY *restore the sofa to its rightful position*). I hate to be patronized and the Chesters always think it's a great favour to allow us to help with their highly connected fair. I wonder you consented, Amy. All right, Aunt March, you can sit down again now.

AMY (*helping to re-settle the ruffled relative*). I am only too willing to help. It's for charity as well as the Chesters, Jo; and I think it very kind of them to let me share the work and the fun. Patronage doesn't trouble me when it is well meant.

AUNT M. Quite right and proper; I like your grateful spirit, my dear; it's always a pleasure to help people who appreciate one's efforts. Some don't, and that is trying. (*She looks disapprovingly at* JO.)

Jo. I don't like favours; they oppress me, and make me feel like a slave. I'd rather do everything for myself, and be perfectly independent.

Aunt C. *(after a pause)*. You have been studying French, have you not, my dear? How are you getting on with it?

Amy. Pretty well, thank you, Aunt Carrol. Aunt March very kindly lets me talk to her French maid as often as I like. It has been such a help with my pronunciation.

Aunt C. How are you about languages, Jo?

Jo. Don't know a word. I'm very stupid about studying anything, and I can't bear French; it's such a slippery, silly sort of language.

Aunt C. Aunt March tells me that you are still persevering with your drawing and painting, Amy.

Amy. Oh, yes, I intend to work very hard this coming winter, so that I may perfect my style and be ready for Rome whenever that joyful time arrives.

Aunt M. Good girl! You deserve to go; and I'm sure that you will some day.

(Mr. *and* Mrs. March *enter from the hall*.)

Mrs. M. Please forgive us for leaving you, but Mr. Laurence asked us to walk with him as far as his front door and we could not refuse him. I hope the girls have been keeping you amused?

Aunt M. Oh, they have.

Mr. M. You will take tea with us, of course?

Aunt. C. Thank you, my dears, but I'm afraid we cannot, for we are expected at Mrs. Chester's. We stayed only to say au revoir, and—

Aunt M. Have a little chat with the girls.

Mrs. M. Oh, what a pity! Well, as soon as Uncle is feeling better, Aunt Carrol, you must bring him to see us before you leave on your travels. You know that you are always welcome, Aunt March.

Aunt M. Thank you for the timely reassurance, Margaret! Well, I have no doubt that you and Arthur are quite capable of seeing us to the carriage, so Amy and Josephine may as well stay here and make themselves useful dismantling all this—this—festoonery. Good-bye for now, girls, our little talk—was enlightening—most enlightening!

(Aunt March *turns on her heel and goes out.* Aunt Carrol, *with a quick* "Good-bye" *to* Jo *and* Amy, *follows, accompanied by* Mr. *and* Mrs. March. Jo *and* Amy *turn back into the room and start to take down the offending garlands.*)

Jo. In other words, dear Aunt March wants to discuss something mighty private with Mother and Father which the "children" mustn't hear! Oh well, I suppose we may as well do as the crotchety old thing suggests; but it does seem a pity to take down your decorations after all the time and trouble you took to make and hang them.

Amy. Never mind; they have served their purpose if they have helped to make Meg's wedding a little more stylish—even if it was a very quiet one.

Jo. The ceremony was certainly very quiet—I suppose we were all too near to tears to make a sound—but the luncheon was the exact opposite! Everyone laughing and talking at once; I would never have believed that so small a group of people could have made such a hubble-bubble of noise! I had a long chin-wag with Aunt Carrol about their trip to Europe. They're going to have an absolutely wonderful time. Just to hear about the places they will be visiting makes it sound like something out of the "Arabian Nights" come true. All those cities and countries that I've read and dreamed about for years—actually coming to life for them. To think that they're really going to be there—walking about in them, experiencing them, meeting all sorts of interesting and exciting people!

Amy. They go first to London, don't they?

Jo. Yes, then on to Paris and Vienna and Rome, of course; then they're to have several weeks in the South of France and—oh, I can hardly bear to talk about it! If I were Cousin Florence, I am sure I should be delirious with excitement. Oh, how I envy her!

Amy. I do, too. They are going to be away for months and months. Just think of all the magnificent art galleries they will be visiting, and all the picturesque scenery and old buildings they will be seeing—just crying out to be sketched and painted.

Jo. Yes, I know how much it would mean to you to see all the fine pictures and sculptures, and to be busy with your pencil and drawing-pad; but for me it would mean such a lot more—something deeper, that I could perhaps put into my writing. I feel that my work is starting to get stagnant for the want of new ideas. More than anything else, I want to travel, Amy, and see something of the wide world about which I have read so much, but of which I have seen so little.

Amy. Well, perhaps we'll be able to go some day, Jo, and carry out all the plans we've made. But, if not, I suppose we must settle down here and make the best of it—and I shall have to take to teaching drawing for my living!

Jo. I can't see you doing that! You hate hard work. You're much more likely to marry some rich man and live in the lap of luxury for the rest of your days.

Amy. Your predictions sometimes come to pass, but I don't believe that one will. I'm sure I wish it would, for if I can't be an artist myself, I should like to be able to help those who are.

Jo. Hmmm! Well, if you wish it, it'll probably come true—your wishes have a way of getting granted.

(BETH *enters, carrying a large tray of tea things. She halts in the archway and looks around in surprise.*)

Beth. Oh, aren't Aunt March and Aunt Carrol staying to tea?

Amy. No, apparently they are due at Mrs. Chester's. Mother and Father are just seeing them off.

Jo (*at the window*). It's certainly taking a long time. Christopher Columbus! They're still talking out there! The aunts sitting in the carriage nodding their heads, and poor Mother and Father standing on the path. How glum they all look! What can they be on about?

AMY (*gathering up the garlands*). There, that's finished! Now, I'm going to put these in the hall for the time being. (*To* BETH.) I suppose there is a terrible pile of washing-up to be done?

BETH. Yes, there is rather a lot. I think Hannah would be glad of some help after tea.

AMY. In that case I'm going up to change at once, for I'm not going to tackle dirty dishes in these clothes. (*She deposits the garlands out of sight in the hall, and proceeds upstairs.*)

BETH. We shan't need all these cups if it is only going to be the family. What was that you were saying about wishes as I came in, Jo?

JO. Oh, it was just some nonsense with Amy. We'd been saying how much we envy Cousin Florence going to Europe; Amy, because she wants to wallow in the art treasures of the old world as she calls it; and I, because I am sure it would be such a tremendous help with my writing.

BETH. Are you still having trouble with your novel, Jo? You have put such a lot of hard work into it.

JO. I've rewritten it three times! I think that's the trouble; I've been fussing over the thing for so long I really don't know whether it's good, bad or indifferent.

BETH (*loyally*). Well, I think it's just perfect.

JO (*smiling*). I wish Mr. Allen, the publisher, felt the same way! As you know, he will only accept it on the condition that I cut it down to a third of its length, and take out all the parts which I particularly like.

BETH. I wouldn't leave out a word of it, for I am sure you will spoil it if you do. Father says the main theme is well worked out, and that you should wait a while and then submit it again.

JO. No, I must either toss it aside for good, pay for printing it myself, or chop it up to suit purchasers and get what I can for it. Oh dear, fame is a very good thing to have in the house, but cash is much more convenient!

(MR. *and* MRS. MARCH *reappear in the archway. They move into the parlour, smiling at their daughters' merriment, but clearly not quite at ease.*)

MRS. M. (*far from happy at what she has to say*). Father and I have been having a long talk with Aunt Carrol. As you know, she is going abroad next month, and she thinks it would be nice for Florence to have a companion nearer her own age to go with her. Most generously she has suggested taking one of you, and she wants—

JO (*full of joyous anticipation*). Me to go with her!

(*Pause.*)

MRS. M (*quietly*). No, dear, not you; it is to be Amy.

Jo. Oh, but, Mother! She's too young; it's my turn first! I've wanted it for so long—it would do me so much good, and be altogether splendid—I must go!

Mr. M. I'm afraid that is impossible, Jo; your aunt has said, quite decidedly, that she wishes Amy to go, and it is not for us to dictate when she offers such a favour.

Jo. It isn't fair—oh, it isn't fair! (*She is near to tears.*)

Mrs. M. I'm afraid that it was partly your own fault, dear. Aunt Carrol remarked that she regretted your blunt manners and rather too independent spirit. She said that she had thought of asking you, but when you told her that favours burdened you, and that you hated French, she decided not to venture to invite you. She feels that Amy will be more appreciative of any help the trip will give her.

Jo (*dissolving into tears*). Oh, my tongue, my abominable tongue! Why can't I learn to keep it quiet?

Mrs. M. Where is Amy, Beth?

Beth. She is upstairs changing, Marmee.

Mrs. M. Then I will go up and tell her the news. Jo, dear, I wish you could have gone, but there is no hope of it this time, I'm afraid; so try to bear it cheerfully, and don't sadden Amy's pleasure by reproaches or regrets.

Jo. I'll try, Marmee; I'll try not only to seem glad, but to be so, and not grudge her one minute of happiness. But it won't be easy, for it is a dreadful disappointment.

(Mrs. March *pats* Jo *on the shoulder and she and* Mr. March *go off together upstairs.* Jo *breaks down again.*)

Beth (*moving to her*). Oh, Jo, please don't upset yourself so; I know how you must feel but—

Jo. It wouldn't be so bad if it wasn't my own stupid fault. When I think of all the silly, foolish things I said about favours being a burden and—oh, I wish I could box my own ears!

Beth. But what made you say them?

Jo. Well, I know it's childish and perverse, but, you see, Aunt March was there, and we'd had a little upset earlier on; though I try not to, I'm always possessed to burst out with some particularly blunt speech or completely false sentiment in front of her. I just can't help it; she makes me say all sorts of wild things which I don't really mean. It's my doom, I suppose, but I don't seem to be able to stop myself. But, oh dear, I'd go on my knees now to Aunt Carrol, if I could, and humbly beg her to burden me with this favour—just to show her how gratefully I could bear it.

Beth. Jo, dear, I know it's very selfish of me, but I couldn't spare you, and so I'm glad that you are not going away just yet.

(*They smile at each other and embrace. Then* Beth *goes to the piano and starts to play "Home Sweet Home".* Jo *dries her eyes and goes to stand by* Beth *as she starts to sing.*)

BETH. "Be it ever so humble, there's no place like home!
A charm from the skies seems to hallow us there,
Which, seek through the world, ne'er is met with elsewhere."
As JO *joins in, the lights begin gently to fade.*

SCENE 3

Early evening: three months later. As the lights come up HANNAH *is discovered busily lighting a fire. The front-door bell rings and the door is heard to open and close. Before* HANNAH *can get to her feet,* MEG *appears, in the archway. She is looking tired and a little overwrought; her cloak is flung rather carelessly over her shoulders, her bonnet is only loosely tied, and there are wisps of hair straggling out from beneath it. She pulls nervously at her gloves, and is slightly out of breath.*

MEG. Oh, Hannah! Is Mother at home?

HANNAH. Why, Miss Meg, you made me jump! No, she ain't—there's no one in except me. Mr. March is at a church meeting, and your Ma and the girls are gone into town. They'll not be long, I reckon. What's the matter, my lamb? You're all of a tremble; here, come and sit down and tell old Hannah all about it. (*She draws* MEG *over to sit on the sofa.*) There, now, that's better.

MEG. Oh, Hannah, I am so tired, and hot, and cross, and worried! Everything is in such an awful mess—I shall never get straight in time, and there's no dinner and John will be here in a minute and he'll be cross, I'm sure. I wonder if you can tell me what it is I've done wrong. I've tried everything I can think of, and it—

HANNAH. Now, now, dearie! I can't follow you. What's amiss? (*A sudden suspicion seizing her.*) Has that Mr. Brooke been beating you, then? Why, I'll—

MEG. No, Hannah, no, of course not! It's the black-currant jelly!

HANNAH. The what?

MEG. The black-currant jelly. You see, John is very fond of currant jelly, and, as we have a good crop of late currants in the garden, I thought how splendid it would be to make some and bottle it to put in the preserve cupboard for use in the winter.

HANNAH. But, of course. What could be nicer? It's easy enough to do —you've seen me at it hundreds of times.

MEG. But, Hannah, that's just it! It's not easy enough to do! I've been at it all day. I picked the currants this morning, then I washed them and boiled them, and strained them, and fussed over them. I did my best; I looked it all up in Mrs. Cornelius' Recipe Book. Then I re-boiled them, and re-sugared them, and re-strained them. I've racked my brains to try to remember what it is you do that I have left un-done. But the more I do the worse it becomes, and try as I will the dreadful stuff just won't "jell". (*She dissolves into tears.*)

HANNAH. There, there! Land sakes, it's not the end of the world! I'll come down with you at once, and see what I can do to put matters to rights.

MEG. Oh, would you? The kitchen's topsy-turvy, I'm afraid, and everything's in confusion. I upset one pan of currants and ruined one of my best aprons—and just look at my hands! (*She pulls off her gloves to reveal heavily stained fingers and hands. At this moment* JOHN BROOKE, *looking anxious, appears suddenly in the archway.*)

JOHN. My dearest girl, what is the matter? Has anything dreadful happened?

HANNAH (*rising*). Ah! Here's your man! Now, I'll just put things to rights in my kitchen before I come down to see to yours. (*As she goes off.*) She's all right, Mister John! Don't you worry yourself!

JOHN. I found the house empty, the back door open, and everything in disorder. There was something burning in a pan on the stove, but no sign of you anywhere. I thought there must have been an accident, or, perhaps, bad news from here had called you away suddenly.

MEG. Oh, John!

JOHN. Tell me quick, then. Don't cry; I can bear anything better than that. Out with it, love.

MEG. You know I was going to make you some currant jelly today?

JOHN. Yes.

MEG. Well, the jelly won't "jell", and I don't know how to make it!

JOHN (*laughing with relief*). Is that all? My dear, fling it out of the window, and don't bother any more about it. I'll buy you quarts if you want it; but for heaven's sake, dry your tears and come home. Now, I've a surprise for you. I've brought Jack Scott home to dinner. I left him in the parlour while I came to look for you, so we'd better hurry back or he'll be—

MEG (*her tears stopping abruptly*). You have brought a man home to dinner, and the house in an uproar? Oh, John, how could you do such a thing?

JOHN. But you have always told me that I was free to bring a friend home to dinner whenever I liked.

MEG. You ought to have sent word, or told me this morning—and you ought to have remembered how busy I was.

JOHN. I forgot about the confounded jelly, and there was no time to send word, for it was only this afternoon, when he called to see me, that I asked him to join us. Anyway, I never thought of asking leave when you have told me so many times that I may ask whom I please when I please, for there would always be a good dinner and a warm welcome waiting. I've never tried it before, and hang me if ever I do again!

MEG. I should hope not! Take him away at once; I can't see him, and there isn't any dinner—good or otherwise.

JOHN. Well, I like that! What's happened to the joint of beef and the vegetables that were ordered in? And what about the special pudding you promised?

MEG. I hadn't time to cook anything; I thought we might dine with Mother—I'm sorry, John, but I was so busy and worried with it all.

JOHN (*his voice softening as he puts his arm around her*). Never mind, it's all a bit of a scrape, I know; but Jack and I will lend a hand to put things straight and we'll have a good time together yet. Don't cry, dear, but just see if you can exert yourself a little bit more, and knock us up something to eat. We're both as hungry as hunters, so we shan't mind what it is. Give us cold meat and bread and cheese—we won't ask for jelly.

MEG (*pushing him angrily aside*). Oh! You must get yourself out of this "bit of a scrape" as best you can. I'm too used up to "exert" myself for anyone. It's like a man to propose something vulgar like bread and cheese for company. I won't have anything of the sort in my house. You can tell Jack Scott that I'm away—sick, dead, anything! I won't see him, and you can both laugh at me and my jelly as much as you like, for there is nothing else to offer him.

(*For a moment* JOHN *seems about to reply, then suddenly he turns on his heel and leaves the room. A second later we hear the front door slam.* MEG *looks after him in dismay; recovering herself she moves to the archway and calls his name, but the word dies on her lips, and she dissolves once more into tears.* HANNAH *reappears from the kitchen and moves across to comfort her.*)

HANNAH. Come now, my pet, don't take on so. I couldn't help but hear some part of what went on, but don't let it upset you—why, you'll be laughing about it tomorrow, you'll see. Now, we'll away to the kitchen. I have the kettle on the boil and we'll see what we can do to clean all this stain off these pretty fingers, and then we'll make you a cup of good strong tea—

(*They go into the kitchen. The front door is heard opening.* MRS. MARCH, JO, *and* BETH, *in outdoor clothes and carrying a few small parcels, appear in the archway.* BETH *is looking very tired and pale; throughout the scene she remains quiet and rather withdrawn.*)

MRS. M (*as she enters*). Ah, home again! My goodness, we have got a lot done this afternoon, haven't we? Beth, dear, you're looking dreadfully tired; I hope it hasn't all been too much for you?

BETH (*forcing a smile*). No, Marmee, I'm all right. I've a slight headache, that's all, but I don't suppose that I'm any more tired than you are.

MRS. M. Oh, I'm sorry, my dear; now, you slip off your bonnet and cloak and lie down quietly on the sofa until dinner-time. (*Putting her hand on* BETH's *forehead as she takes her bonnet and cloak.*) Your forehead is very warm—are you feeling feverish?

BETH. No, please don't worry, Marmee; I'm all right—really. I'll have a little rest and then I shall feel fine.

JO (*picking up a letter from the mantelpiece*). Oh, the afternoon post has come! Here's another letter from Amy—and, look, it's got a different sort of stamp on it! They must have gone on to France at last. May I open it, Marmee?

MRS. M. (*settling* BETH *on the sofa*). Yes, Jo, we must hear what fresh adventures she's had. Is that comfortable, Beth? All ready to have the latest report from our foreign correspondent?

BETH. Yes, thank you; I feel much better already.

MRS. M. (*taking the letter from* Jo). Thank you, dear; now, what has our Amy got to say this time! Yes, it's from Paris!

"Dearest People,

"In my last letter I told you about our stay in London—"

(HANNAH *enters from the kitchen*.)

HANNAH. Excuse me, mum, but might I just have a word with you?

MRS. M. Why, yes, Hannah. What is it?

HANNAH. It's Miss Meg; there's been a little—er—difference, if you understand me, between her and Mister John. She's out in the kitchen at the moment, and I think she'd like to see you before she comes in here.

MRS. M. Why, of course, I'll come at once. Jo dear, you finish reading the letter, will you?

HANNAH. It's nothing to be bothered about, mum; it was only a little tiff and they're going to have that wonderful a time making it up!

(HANNAH *and* MRS. MARCH *go out*.)

(Jo *picks up the letter and glances briefly through it. An expression of disappointment crosses her face, which does not escape* BETH.)

BETH. Has Amy any special news?

Jo (*passing her the letter*). No, it's just a short letter to say that they have arrived safely, and then she goes drooling on describing art galleries and elegant young men who have been paying her attention and twirling their blond moustaches at her. As if anyone was the slightest bit interested! She even includes a fashion note on the Empress of France, who, according to our Amy, dresses in "horrid taste". I do wish instead that she'd describe the places she's visiting with a little more detail—that would be interesting!

BETH. Poor Jo! The disappointment of not going still hurts, doesn't it?

Jo. Just a little at times, but I try not to let it show!

BETH. Never mind, your turn will come, you'll see! Now you've had one novel published you'll be able to get others accepted, and then you'll soon be rich and famous and able to go where you will!

Jo. Dear Beth, you do try to keep our spirits up, don't you? But I don't know if I shall ever have the heart to write another novel, now.

BETH. Whatever do you mean, Jo?

Jo. Well, everyone said that the professional criticism I should receive when my book was published would be a help and guide to my future writing. But it was all so contradictory that I don't know whether I have written a promising book or broken the ten commandments!

BETH. Yes, it was a bit bewildering.
JO. It certainly was—and I still haven't quite recovered! One paper said that it was "an exquisite book, full of truth, beauty, and earnestness; all is sweet, pure, and healthy" and another that the "theory of the book was bad—full of morbid fancies, spiritualistic ideas, and unnatural characters". Ah well, I suppose the joke is on my side for the parts that were taken straight out of real life were denounced as impossible and absurd; and the scenes that I made up out of my own silly head were pronounced "Charmingly natural, tender, and true"! So I'll comfort myself with that; and, perhaps, later on, I'll up again and try another!

(MRS. MARCH *re-enters from the kitchen.*)

BETH. How is Meg, Marmee?

MRS. M. It's all right, my dears, nothing to worry about. She's just a little upset, that's all; at the moment she's helping Hannah prepare dinner, and I think that something to occupy her attention is a good thing. (*To* BETH.) Now, how is the headache?

BETH. Better, thank you; but I think I'll go up and bathe my forehead with rose-water. It will help to soothe the pain, and freshen me up a little, too.

MRS. M. That's a good idea; there is a fresh bottle in my medicine cabinet if you need it.

BETH. If I may, I'll take Amy's letter up with me to read.

MRS. M. By all means, my dear, Father and I will read it together after dinner.

(BETH *goes slowly upstairs.* MRS. MARCH *watches her anxiously for several moments and then turns back into the room. There is a pause.*)

JO (*with an effort*). Marmee, I've something rather special about which I want to talk to you.

MRS. M. What is it, Jo?

JO. I want to go away somewhere this winter for a change.

MRS. M. I see; and what have you in mind, my dear?

JO. I want to do something new; I feel restless, and anxious to be seeing, doing and learning more than I am. I brood too much over my own small affairs, and I think I need stirring up. So, if I can be spared this winter, I'd like to hop a little way and try my wings.

MRS. M. And where will you hop?

JO (*warming to her theme*). To New York. I had a bright idea yesterday. Your old friend Mrs. Kirke mentioned when she wrote to you that she was looking for someone who would act as a sort of governess for her children, and take on the family sewing. Well, I think I might do very well at that, if she would have me.

MRS. M. I am certain she would have you. But are you sure you want to go out to service in that great boarding-house?

JO. It's not exactly going out to service, for Mrs. Kirke is our friend and the kindest soul that ever lived. She would make things pleasant for me, I know, and her family is separate from the rest of the house. It's honest work and I'd not be ashamed of it.

Mrs. M. Nor I; but what about your writing?

Jo. All the better for a change! I shall see and hear new things, get new ideas, and, even if I don't get much time to write whilst I'm there, I shall come home with quantities of material for my scribbling.

Mrs. M. I've no doubt of it; but are these your only reasons for this sudden fancy?

(Pause.)

Jo. No, Mother.

Mrs. M. May I know the others?

(A further pause, and then Jo speaks with unaccustomed embarrassment.)

Jo. It may be vain and wrong to say it, but, well, I'm afraid—that Laurie is getting too fond of me.

Mrs. M. Then you don't care for him in the way it is evident that he begins to care for you?

Jo. Mercy, no! I am fond of him, as I have always been, and I'm immensely proud of him, but as for anything more, it's out of the question.

Mrs. M. Well, I'm glad of that, Jo!

Jo *(rather surprised)*. Why, please?

Mrs. M. Because, dear, I don't think you are suited to one another. As friends, you are very happy; but I fear you would both rebel if you were together for life. You are too much alike and too fond of freedom, not to mention quick tempers and strong wills, to get on happily together in a relationship which needs both patience and forbearance, as well as love.

Jo. That's just the feeling I had, though I couldn't express it. I'm glad you think that he is only beginning to care for me. It would bother me dreadfully to make him unhappy, but I can't fall in love with him merely out of gratitude.

Mrs. M. You are sure of his feelings for you?

Jo. I'm afraid so, Mother; he hasn't said anything, but he looks a great deal. I think I'd better go away before it comes to anything.

Mrs. M. I agree with you, and I will write to Mrs. Kirke this evening.

Jo. Let us say nothing about it to Laurie until everything is settled, then I'll run away before he can collect his wits and be tragical. He's been through so many little trials of this sort since he's been at college that he must be used to it, and will soon get over his love-lornity. *(She chuckles to herself.)* I was just thinking how shocked Aunt March would be if she knew you were helping to discourage the attentions of a wealthy young suitor—"an admirable alliance", as she would call it.

Mrs. M. Perhaps she would, but I desire only to see my children happy. Meg is so—for what has happened this evening is nothing and will be quickly forgotten—and I am content with her success. You I leave to enjoy your liberty, till you tire of it, for only then will you find that there is something sweeter. Amy is my chief care now, but good sense will help her. For Beth, at present, I indulge no hopes except that she may be well and grow daily stronger.

Jo. I know what! She must take Laurie in hand after I'm gone! She can pet and comfort him, and so help cure him of this romantic notion.

(MEG *reappears from the kitchen. She is calm now, but still low-spirited. She pauses almost shyly in the archway.*)

MRS. M. Come in, Meg dear! Would you like to stay and have dinner with us?

MEG. No, thank you, Mother; I think I ought to go home.

MRS. M. Yes, dear, perhaps you should—it would be the wise thing to do.

MEG. Oh, Mother, I am so ashamed—it was all so petty and silly—and I am more sorry than I can say that it should have happened here. Please forgive me.

MRS. M. My dear, there is nothing for me to forgive. It is from John that you must ask forgiveness.

MEG. Yes, I know that. This is the very first time that we have had cross words, and I was the one who really started it.

MRS. M. Well, it may not be the last time, but I think you have learnt one lesson, Meg, if you are ready to admit that you are in the wrong. You must guard against these little piques and misunderstandings, for they so often pave the way for bitter sorrow and regret. John is a good man, my dear, and he loves you very dearly. Be careful not to spoil that love with foolish quarrels or hasty words.

MEG. I'll remember, Mother; it was only that—

(*The front-door bell rings.*)

MRS. M. Something tells me that that is John come to say that he is sorry, too, and to take you home. Now, Jo, you and I will let him in, and then we have the table to lay for dinner, have we not? (*With a smile and a kiss for* MEG.) I'll say "good night" now, my dear, for when we have finished I expect you'll be gone, won't you?

(MRS. MARCH *and* JO *go out. There is the sound of subdued voices and then silence. After a slight pause* JOHN *appears in the archway. For a moment nothing is said.*)

JOHN (*moving to the window*). I think we are going to have a new moon, my dear.

MEG (*sitting at end of sofa*). I have no objection.

JOHN. The evenings are drawing in, are they not?

MEG. Yes, we shall soon have the winter with us.

JOHN (*sitting at the opposite end of sofa*). Jack Scott has excused himself, but says he hopes he may call to see us again some time.

MEG. But, of course, do invite him any time; I shall be more than delighted to see him. There will always be a good dinner and a warm welcome—

Suddenly she becomes conscious of her own words, and they die away. She steals a glance at JOHN *and finds him looking at her and smiling; for a moment she hesitates, then she starts to smile, too. Seeing this,* JOHN *takes heart, the smile broadens to a laugh, and gently he slides his hand along the sofa towards her.* MEG *starts to laugh, too, as she stretches out her hand towards him.*

CURTAIN

ACT TWO

SCENE I

An afternoon in the late spring of the following year. AUNT MARCH *is being entertained to tea. She and* BETH *are listening to* MRS. MARCH, *who is reading aloud from a letter.* BETH *is looking more frail than ever.*

MRS. M. "... the time passes very quickly, for there is always so much to be done—what with lessons for the children and my various other duties. Mrs. Kirke has been more than kind to me during these last seven months, and it hardly seems possible that I have been here so long or that, before another month is over, I shall be home with you once again."

AUNT M. Hmm! So Josephine will be home next month! Well, I shall look forward to seeing what improvement the change has made in her; though it does not seem to me that a winter spent as a governess in a boarding-house in New York can offer much in the way of refinement.

BETH. Oh, but, Aunt March, I think she has loved every minute of it. She has been working with children, which is a great joy to her; and she has made new friends amongst her fellow boarders, about whom she has written to us in great detail. Do read the bit about Mr. Bhaer, Marmee.

MRS. M. "I shall be very sorry, of course, to say 'good-bye' to Mrs. Kirke and the children, but the person whom I am most going to miss when I leave New York will be Professor Bhaer, who has been such a wonderful friend to me all the time I have been here."

AUNT M. Oh, he is that impoverished German school-teacher whom she has mentioned before, is he not? Well, go on, Margaret, go on! What are you waiting for? What more does she have to say about him?

MRS. M. "He is in no respect fascinating, imposing, or brilliant, and yet people gather around him as naturally as they gather about a warm hearth. He is no longer young, but he is as happy-hearted as a boy. He is plain and odd, yet he has a definite charm of his own, which is, perhaps, best summed up in one word—benevolence. For he is truly benevolent in the nicest possible way. Well, I must bring this scribble-scrabble letter to a close; on reading it over it strikes me as being rather full of Mr. Bhaer, but, as you know, I am always interested in odd people! It's all right, Marmee, he must be almost forty—so there's no harm in it! Heaps of love to everyone and bless you all! Ever your loving Jo."

AUNT M. A choice companion, I must say! She seems uncommonly interested in him; though he does not sound to me to be an ideal friend for a niece of mine.

MRS. M. I think you forget, Aunt March, that Jo is a grown-up young woman now, and quite capable of making her own way in the world. Both her father and I feel that she has good common sense, particularly in such matters as the selection of friends.

AUNT M. That's as may be! Trust Josephine to select the most unlikely person in the household! Indeed, I am not at all sure that friendship with a middle-aged foreigner is altogether desirable for a girl of Josephine's age.

MRS. M. I do not think there is anything undesirable about it, Aunt. They are fellow boarders in the same house, and both engaged in teaching; it is only natural that there should be a common bond between them. My old friend Mrs. Kirke has written of Mr. Bhaer in glowing terms, and he is apparently well liked and respected by all who know him.

BETH. And did you know that Jo is sufficiently impressed to have undertaken German lessons with him? Though she has always found foreign languages a great trial.

AUNT M. German lessons, indeed! Mercy on us! Then some good may come from it after all—though I have my doubts. I seem to remember your sister telling me rather forcibly once that she couldn't bear French and was very stupid about studying languages. That reminds me; how is Amy? Still cavorting about in the South of France, I suppose?

MRS. M. Yes, she is having a truly wonderful time. They have spent most of the winter in Nice, and seem to be staying on there indefinitely. I think the climate suits Uncle Carrol. But Amy has written to you from there, has she not?

AUNT M. Oh, yes, I have had several letters full of ecstatic descriptions —and French expressions which I did not clearly understand. I have no doubt that the trip is doing her a power of good. Apart from her drawing and painting, on which she is as busily engaged as ever, she seems to be meeting some very eligible young men. She has had much to say about a young Englishman, called Vaughan, who has been paying her a good deal of attention. I gather from Mary that he is a very wealthy young man with a most satisfactory background. There is also a Polish count, whom she met at a ball—

MRS. M. Yes, Amy has told us about them, too. She is impressionable, and I sincerely hope that so many attentions and gallantries in such romantic surroundings will neither turn her head nor blur her judgment.

AUNT M. Upon my word, Margaret! You do not appear to have any real ambition for your girls! I assume that you would like Amy to make a good match if she had the chance?

MRS. M. Assuredly, but only if it means that she is to be truly happy in a good man's love.
(BETH *has a sudden fit of coughing.*)
AUNT M. That is a nasty cough you have, child. Are you taking anything for it?
BETH. Yes, thank you, Aunt March. Marmee has made up a syrup for me which is very soothing.
MRS. M. That very bad cold Beth had during the winter seems to have left her with this cough, which she cannot quite shake off, I'm afraid. The doctor has prescribed the syrup, and I think it is giving some ease, is it not, my dear?
BETH. Oh yes, Marmee, it doesn't keep me awake at night as it did.
AUNT M. Well, that is good. Now, what is the latest news about Meg? After all, that is really why I have come. Her baby is due this week, is it not?
MRS. M. Yes, the doctor says either tomorrow or the day after.
AUNT M. So soon! And why did she not come home here to have the child, where she could be properly looked after, may I ask?
MRS. M. Naturally I wanted her to come, but she would not hear of it. She said that it would mean a lot of trouble and upset for the family—as if that would worry any of us; but, most of all, she feels that it will make "Dovecote" a real home if her first baby is born there.
AUNT M. Mercy on us! Marriage doesn't seem to have got rid of any of the foolish, romantic notions that fill that girl's head! Then who is looking after her?
MRS. M. Hannah. She has gone to stay there for a week or two until it is all over and Meg is up and about again.
AUNT M. I suppose that Hannah is reliable, and knows what she is about?
MRS. M. Well, Aunt March, she came to be with me when Meg was born, and helped also to bring Jo, Beth, and Amy into the world—so she is not without experience! Certainly no one could be more interested in or concerned about Meg's baby, and I declare that she would be most hurt if she were not in charge. I go down at least twice a day to see that all is well, and do what I can to help. I was there this morning, and Meg was looking bonny. I usually go down about this time in the afternoon. Would you care to accompany me today?
AUNT M. Yes, I think I will. I am naturally anxious that all should be going smoothly for the arrival of my first great-great-nephew.
MRS. M. But, Aunt, there can be no guarantee that it will be a boy.
AUNT M. Not a boy! But it must be a boy! I shall be seriously put about if it is not. After all, Margaret, you were able to furnish me only with nieces—I look to Meg to rectify that state of affairs.
MRS. M. But, Aunt March—

AUNT M. But me no "buts", Margaret! And I wish to hear no more talk of female offspring. Now, let us proceed to the "Pigeon-loft" or whatever that poky little house is called.
MRS. M. "Dovecote", Aunt March. (*Nervously.*) Forgive me for saying this, but just as things are at this time, you—well, you won't say anything that might upset Meg, will you?
AUNT M. Well, upon my soul! What are you suggesting? Am I likely to say anything that would upset anyone?

(*The front door opens and closes loudly, and* HANNAH, *her cap askew, her hair awry, clutching her shawl about her shoulders, appears breathlessly in the archway.*)

HANNAH. Oh, mum! It's happened! It's all over!
MRS. M. Hannah! You mean the baby? It's arrived?
HANNAH. Yes, everything's just fine, mum! But wait till I tell you!
AUNT M. Is it a boy or a girl?
MRS. M. But when, Hannah? This morning there was no sign—
BETH. How wonderful! Is Meg all right?
HANNAH. About an hour since. I had no chance to send word; it was all so sudden. I've left Lotty there now to look after things, while I ran up to let you know that—
AUNT M. Yes, Yes! But what is it—a boy or a girl?
MRS. M. (*gathering up her shawl*). I'll come at once, Hannah. How is Meg? Is she all right? Is there anything you need?
HANNAH. She's fine, mum, lying there so pretty as a picture, and so proud, because, you see—
MRS. M. Get your shawl, Beth; we must go at once. You will come, won't you, Aunt March?
AUNT M. Of course I'm coming! But I want to know is it a boy or a girl?
HANNAH. You wait till Mister John gets home! He's going to be that proud, I tell you. Fancy to be—
MRS. M. Have you enough of everything you need down there, Hannah? Milk, eggs?
HANNAH. Oh, there's enough to feed a regiment! No one's going to be hungry, though there are—
AUNT M. (*banging her cane on the floor*). I demand to know, woman, is it a boy or a girl?
HANNAH. Bless you, mum, I've been trying to tell you. It's both! She's had twins!

MRS. MARCH, HANNAH *and* BETH *embrace each other in an ecstasy of joy, whilst* AUNT MARCH *sits transfixed, her face a study in blank amazement. The lights fade quickly.*

Scene 2

*A month later; early evening. The family—*MOTHER, FATHER, MEG, JOHN, *and* BETH—*are gathered around* JO *on her first evening at home. She is looking extremely well, and is busy regaling the others with stories of her adventures in New York.*

MRS. M. Well, Jo, it is obvious that you haven't lost your flair for making whatever happens to you into a very funny story when you relate it afterwards! It is lovely having you home again—if only to make us all laugh!

JO. Oh, Marmee, it is so good to be home again—I've missed you all so dreadfully! Today, in the train, the wheels kept saying to me "You're-going-home! You're-going-home! You're-going-home! You're-going-home!" and when I caught sight of all of you on the platform I could hardly wait for the train to stop before leaping out!

MR. M. You cannot have missed us any more than we have missed you, my dear, for the house has been very quiet without you!

BETH. Oh, yes! It has been just like the days when you used to shut yourself up in your little attic-study to write away at your novel, and we used never to hear a sound from you from morning till night.

MRS. M. That reminds me, Jo, did you manage to do any writing whilst you were in New York? You never mentioned it in your letters, and I forgot to ask when I wrote to you.

JO. Oh, Mother! Father! I have a confession to make about that, and I may as well clear my mind of it straight away. Yes, I have been writing, but nothing of which you would be proud, and something of which I am now rather ashamed.

MRS. M. Jo, dear, what do you mean?

JO. Well, I tried my hand at these sensation stories which appear in the cheap papers. I was told that editors paid well for such things, so I concocted as "thrilling" a tale as I could manage and offered it to the "Weekly Volcano", just to see—

MEG. The "Weekly Volcano"? But that is a dreadful paper, Jo! Lotty had a copy in the kitchen the other day and the illustrations were really terrifying.

JO. Yes, I knew you'd be shocked. Well, anyway, they accepted my first effort, and asked if I could do one a week at twenty-five dollars a time. It was too big a temptation, I'm afraid; I did so want to earn some money so that I should be able to bring you home nice presents, and perhaps have enough to take Beth for a little holiday in the mountains—oh, and lots of other things. So I accepted the offer, and was busy scribbling away about all sorts of dark deeds for a good many weeks.

JOHN. But wherever did you get the ideas for your plots? These "sensation" stories are usually decidedly harrowing and bloodthirsty.

Jo. Well, I searched the newspapers for accidents, incidents and crimes; and I'm afraid I aroused the suspicions of attendants in the public libraries by asking for books on all manner of poisons and treasons. (*Seeing the changed expressions on the faces of her parents.*) Oh, I know it was wrong. Not only was I becoming absorbed with all sorts of unhealthy thoughts, but, worse still, I was providing morbid amusement for others. I couldn't see it at first; I thought that, as there must be a demand for it, there was no harm in supplying it.

BETH. What made you think differently, Jo?

Jo. It was something Mr. Bhaer said when he came across a similar paper in the house one day—luckily it wasn't the "Weekly Volcano" with one of my stories—but what he said applied just the same.

BETH. And what did he say?

Jo. He said that such stories were trash, and that if the people who wrote them knew what harm they did, they would not feel that their living was honest.

MR. M. I could not agree with him more.

Jo (*moving to him*). Oh, Father, I know, and I am truly sorry; but, until then, I didn't realize what harm I'd been doing. Mr. Bhaer, without knowing it, made me see the error of my ways.

MEG. So what did you do?

Jo. I made a great bonfire of everything I had written, and turned my back on that branch of literature once and for all. I've decided that, as far as writing is concerned, I don't know anything! I'll wait until I do before I try again, and, in the meantime, sweep the streets if necessary—that's honest, anyway!

MEG. What is this Mr. Bhaer of yours like, Jo?

Jo. Now, Meg, don't be arch! He isn't at all that kind of friend. You ought to know me better than that! Besides, I've written and told you all about him in my letters.

MEG. Well, yes: but you haven't given us a very clear picture of his appearance.

Jo. Oh, his appearance! Well, that might not appeal to you so very much! He is a regular German—rather stout, with brown hair tumbled all over his head, a bushy beard, a droll nose and the kindest eyes I ever saw. His clothes are always untidy, and he hasn't a handsome feature in his face except his beautiful teeth. But one can't help liking him for he— (*She becomes suddenly aware of the amused glances which the others are exchanging, and breaks off.*)

JOHN. Well, I, for one, should like to meet your professor from Berlin, Jo; but what an odd name! I dare not think what Aunt March would make of it!

Jo. Now, don't laugh at his horrid name; it isn't pronounced either "Bear" or "Beer", but something between the two, as only Germans can say it. (*Taking up a book, wrapped in brown paper, from among a number of small parcels which have been tumbled on to the table.*) Look,

he gave me this as a parting gift. (*She unwraps a finely bound volume.*)
MRS. M. Jo! What a beautifully bound book! (*Taking it from her and reading the title.*) "The Complete Works of William Shakespeare." This is indeed a handsome present, my dear.
Jo. Yes, isn't it? It was his own copy, and one he valued very much, so you may imagine how I felt when he gave it to me. (*Opening it.*) See, he has written inside. Read it aloud, Marmee.
MRS. M. "For Josephine March, you say often that you wish you had a library; here I give you one, for between these two lids . . ."
Jo. He means "covers".
MRS. M. ". . . are many books in one. The study of character herein will help you to read it in the world, and paint it with your pen. From your friend Friedrich Bhaer." (*Closing the book and returning it to Jo.*) That is charming, Jo; and extremely generous of him.
Jo. I hope that you will all know him better one day, for I have asked him to call and see us if he ever travels this way. He said he would try, but he did not know when that might be. Well, the winter's gone, and I've written no books, and earned no fortune; but I've made a friend worth having, and I'll try to keep him all my life. But that's quite enough about me for the time being! Now, let me have some of your news! Meg, how are those wonderful babies of yours? I can hardly wait to see them! When Marmee wrote to say that you had had twins I was never more staggered in my life!
JOHN. According to Meg, they are the most remarkable children you ever saw.
MEG. And so they are, John! (*To Jo.*) I don't like leaving them for a minute, but Hannah insisted on looking after them this evening so that we might all meet and welcome you home as a family. Tomorrow you are to come to lunch and be formally presented!
Jo. That will be fun! What names are you going to give them?
MEG. The boy is to be John Laurence and the little girl we are going to call Margaret.
JOHN. After her mother and grandmother. But we shall call her Daisy, so as not to have two Megs.
MEG. We were going to call the mannie Jack, but Laurie had the bright suggestion that we name him Demijohn, and Demi for short.
Jo. Daisy and Demi—just the thing! Trust our Laurie to find the perfect solution! How is Laurie?
(*Pause.*)
MRS. M. He seems to have been taking his studies much more seriously and to have been working harder at college during this last six months. Mr. Laurence tells us that his tutors are all very pleased with him, and that he is expected to do especially well when he graduates next month.
BETH. We are all invited to attend the graduation ceremony and then

we are going to give a special dinner here in his honour when he comes home. I am so glad that you have returned in time for it, Jo.

Jo. Well, I'm pleased to hear that he has been working hard. It sounds as though he has got over his (*For a moment she pauses in confusion.*)—wild pranks and foolishness, and is going to do well. I shall be so proud to see him graduate. What does he plan to do after that?

Mr. M. There has been some talk of his going abroad for a period, but I do not believe that anything has been definitely settled.

Jo. Yes, I think that would be a very good thing for him to do.

Meg (*rising and preparing to leave*). Well, we must be going, for we have left Daisy and Demi quite long enough; I am always fearful that some dreadful disaster has overtaken them in my absence.

John. Don't be a silly goose! What could possibly happen with Hannah there to look after them?

Meg. All the same, we must go, for Hannah will be wanted home here, and, anyway, she has not seen Jo yet. Good-bye for now, Jo dear; it is so good to have you home again; we shall see you tomorrow and have a longer gossip then! (*She kisses Jo, and then her parents and* Beth.) Good night, Mother; good night, Father; good night, Beth.

John. Good night, Jo. We shall look forward to seeing you tomorrow. (*He kisses* Jo.)

Jo. Good night, Meg; good night, John. I am longing to see those babes! (Meg *and* John *go to the front door.*)

Mr. M. Well, Jo, I'll take your boxes and parcels upstairs for you. (*He goes upstairs with boxes, etc.*)

Jo. Oh, thank you, Father; you are a dear.

Beth. And I'll go and make sure that the dinner's all right—we have all your favourite dishes, Jo!

(*She goes quickly to the kitchen.* Mrs. March, *who is collecting up bonnets and shawls, turns quickly on hearing this, and calls after* Beth, *her voice betraying a sudden note of anxiety.*)

Mrs. M. I'm coming, dear; don't go doing too much now.

Jo. Marmee, how tired and ill Beth looks. I didn't like to say anything to her in front of everyone, but surely she is not as well as— Marmee, dear, what is it? What's happened?

Mrs. M. Well, Jo, you have to know sooner or later; I had hoped to spare you until tomorrow, so that I might tell you when you were rested and not tired after your journey; but I suppose it is all too dreadfully apparent to be concealed. I wanted to write and warn you before you came home, but Beth would not hear of it, for she would have nothing to cloud your happy time in New York.

Jo. "Warn" me? About what, Marmee?

Mrs. M. About Beth, dear. You must prepare yourself for some terrible news. I am afraid that she is not going to be with us for very much longer. (*Her voice breaks.*)

Jo. Marmee! You don't mean— You can't mean that she—

Mrs. M. I am afraid so, dear; the doctor says there is nothing more that can be done. This has been coming on for a long time, but her general health has just not been strong enough to fight back. Thank God she is not in any pain; but the disease has too strong a hold on her, and it can only be a matter of months before— (*Her voice falters, and she turns away. After a moment* Mrs. March *recovers and rises and moves to* Jo.) Jo, dear, it is Beth's wish that everything should go on just as if nothing was wrong. She wants these last few months to be happy ones which we may enjoy together. It is not going to be easy, but with your help, and for her sake, your father and I will do our best. It is a great comfort to have you home again, Jo. I always feel strong when you are here. I must go to her now, for she is still inclined to want to do far too much about the house. (*With a quick embrace* Mrs. March *goes to the kitchen.* Beth *reappears.*)

Beth (*brightly, as she enters, seats herself, and takes up her sewing*). Dinner won't be long now, Jo. Marmee has sent me in to rest, and to talk to you whilst she—

Jo. Beth, oh, Beth!

(*She throws her arms about her sister, her own head turned away in grief.* Beth, *realizing instantly what has happened, folds her arms around* Jo, *and holds her close in a gesture of comfort and reassurance. When she speaks again her voice is calm and with a note of serenity that is very near to happiness.*)

Beth. Jo, dear, I'm glad you know, for I wasn't looking forward to telling you. But you mustn't upset yourself like this. I've known for a good while—even before the doctor confirmed it—and now I'm used to it, it isn't so hard to think about or bear. You must try to see it that way, too, and not be troubled about me.

Jo. You knew before I went away last autumn, and have kept it to yourself for so long?

Beth. Yes, I gave up hoping then, but I didn't like to own it. I tried to think that it was just a sick fancy; but when I saw the doctor, after you had gone to New York, I knew I was not mistaken.

Jo. Oh, Beth, you should have written and told me. I would have come home at once to comfort and help you. How could you shut me out, and bear it all alone?

Beth. Perhaps it was wrong, but I tried to do what I thought was right. I didn't want to spoil the happy time you were having in New York, especially after your disappointment in not going to Europe.

Jo. As if that would have mattered compared to this! Beth, you must get well.

Beth. I want to—oh, so much! I try, but every day I seem to lose a little more strength, and grow equally sure that I shall never gain it back. It's like the tide, Jo, when it turns—it goes slowly, but it can't be stopped.

Jo. It shall be stopped—your tide must not turn so soon—nineteen is too young. Beth, I can't let you go. I'll work and pray, and fight against it. There must be ways—it can't be too late. God won't be so cruel as to take you from us.

BETH. I am not clever about these things, and I don't know how to express myself (*With a smile.*)—and shouldn't try to anyone except my old Jo—but I have a feeling that it was never intended that I should live long. I'm not like the rest of you; I never made any plans about what I'd do when I grew up; I never thought of being married, as you all did. I couldn't seem to imagine myself as doing anything but trotting about here at home. I never wanted to go away, and the hard part now is the leaving you all.

Jo. But, Beth, don't give up yet; I am going to believe that it is a sick fancy, and not let you think it's true.

BETH. No, we must be sensible, Jo. Now, I want you to promise me something; you must take my place and be everything to Father and Mother when I'm gone. Meg has John and the babies to comfort her; and Amy has Aunt and Uncle Carrol and Cousin Florence and the distractions of a strange land to take her mind from sad thoughts; but Father and Mother have only you—and they will turn to you, I know—don't fail them.

Jo. But it won't be so soon; you won't be leaving us before Amy's return. Why, she is due back in the spring, and I mean to have you well and rosy to greet her!

BETH. Jo, dear, don't hope any more; it won't do any good, I'm sure of that. But we won't be miserable, for we are going to continue living happily together, and enjoying each other's company while we wait. I am not in pain, and—when the time comes—I think the tide will go out easily, if you help me.

Jo hides her face in the folds of her sister's dress, and BETH *gently caresses the head in her lap as the lights fade.*

SCENE 3

A month later. It is a hot evening in July, and the occasion of the dinner party held in LAURIE'S *honour after his graduation. The lights come up on a stage that is empty only for a moment, for almost immediately* AUNT MARCH, *accompanied by* MR. LAURENCE, *enter from the direction of the dining-room.* AUNT MARCH, *who is in evening dress with many jet ornaments and other pieces of jewellery, is fanning herself vigorously; for her, she is in a remarkably mellow mood.*

AUNT M. (*as she enters*). Upon my word, it is uncomfortably hot this evening.

MR. L. (*leading her to a chair*). Yes, we are having a remarkably warm summer this year.

AUNT M. It is cooler in here, thank goodness! I found the dining-room quite overpowering—especially with all the young people chattering away one across the other like so many demented parrots! Thank you for escorting me in here, Mr. Laurence; at least we shall have a few moments of peace before they burst in on top of us!

MR. L. Well, dear lady, they are naturally full of elation after the exciting events of yesterday. We must allow for a certain liveliness and hilarity on this occasion. It was most generous of your niece and nephew to give this little family dinner in honour of Laurie's graduation. Truly, this is his second home!

AUNT M. The ceremony went well yesterday?

MR. L. Yes, Laurie has fulfilled all my hopes and expectations. I am more proud of him than I can adequately describe. He gave the Latin Oration, you know, and spoke it with all the grace of a Phillips and the eloquence of a Demosthenes. I wish you could have been there to hear him.

AUNT M. I have no great partiality for Latin Orations, but I am glad he did well. Certainly he was well supported by the rest of the March family! Margaret and Arthur; the girls and Mr. Brooke—all there to exult with him and share his hour of glory. But what of his future, sir? Have you any plans?

MR. L. He has expressed a great desire to travel abroad, and I promised that he should do so when he was through college. Naturally, he will take my place in the business in due course—I am merely holding on till he is ready to do so; but I can wait a little longer while he enjoys the holiday he so richly deserves. Besides, whilst he is in London he can attend to some business of ours there that needs looking after; I shall be more than delighted, for, at my age, I am disinclined to leave the comforts of my own home to go voyaging across the ocean!

AUNT M. I was thinking in terms of marriage, Mr. Laurence. What are your plans for him there?

MR. L. Plans? Indeed, I would not dream of intruding in such a personal matter.

AUNT M. But, surely, you are anxious that he should make a suitable match? There must be those of whom you would approve in preference to others?

MR. L. Since you are so pressing, ma'am, I will say this much; though he may have had many flirtations at college, there has only ever been but one girl on whom he has truly set his affections. If she will have him, then my happiness will all but equal his, but it is not for me to interfere by either word or deed. They have known each other for a long time now—indeed, one might almost say that they had grown up together—so they know something of each other's virtues and shortcomings. Jo is a fine, intelligent girl, of whom I think a—

AUNT M. Jo? Do you mean our Josephine?

MR. L. But, of course—who else? I assumed that you must have seen or been told how they—

AUNT M. Told? Nobody ever tells me anything! Well, upon my soul! Those two have always seemed to me to be shouting and jumping about and generally behaving like two ragamuffins; it never occurred to me that—

(*At this point* HANNAH *enters from the kitchen, carrying a tray with coffee-pot, cups, etc.*)

MR. L. Ah, here is the coffee! Well, I think I will just go and tell the others that it is ready, if you will excuse me, ma'am. It will save your legs, Hannah, for I know that you have much to do.

HANNAH. Oh, thank you, sir. (*Having set down the tray, she prepares to leave, but is restrained by a wave from* AUNT MARCH.)

AUNT M. I will have mine right away; I feel I need it—and, in any case, by the time the others come in and get settled it will be stone cold. (HANNAH *looks dubious, but pours a cup of coffee.*) I do like coffee to be quite fresh, and really hot. Not too much milk, now! I hope the coffee has been well ground. Let me see—hmm, yes, a little more milk than that, I think. Now, the sugar—

(JO *enters boisterously.*)

JO. Come on, Aunt March! It's such a lovely warm evening that we're going to have our coffee out on the veranda. Hannah, would you take the tray out, please? Father is going to read aloud to us, and I have to look for a particular book of poems for him.

(HANNAH *returns* AUNT MARCH'S *cup and the sugar to the tray, and briskly goes off with it in the direction of the front door.* AUNT MARCH *is left with her hands still outstretched.* JO *moves to the bookshelves to search for the book of poems.*)

AUNT M. But I wish to have my coffee here! I have no desire to go outside! The evening air is most unhealthy—full of pollutions from the day, and usually seething with enormous mosquitoes.

JO. Not at all, Aunt March, it is a beautiful evening, full of the sweet scent of Father's roses. Besides, it is so much cooler on the veranda.

AUNT M. Mercy on us! No sooner does one get comfortably settled in this house than one is immediately bundled away somewhere else. (*As she leaves.*) However rose-scented the air may be, it is sure to be damp and bad for my rheumatism—

(JO, *looking after her with an amused grin, returns to her search for the book. She has just found it when* LAURIE *appears in the archway.*)

JO. I've found it, Laurie; I was just coming.

LAURIE. Don't go for a moment, Jo. I want to talk to you. I—

JO. No, Laurie, not now, please. We must join the others and—

LAURIE. You must hear me. It's no use, Jo; we've got to have it out, and the sooner the better for both of us.

JO (*sitting reluctantly*). Say what you want to, then; I'll listen.

LAURIE. I've loved you ever since I've known you, Jo—I couldn't help it—and I've tried to show it, but you wouldn't let me; now I'm going to make you hear, and give me an answer, for I can't go on like this any longer.

JO. I wanted to save you this; I thought you'd understand—

LAURIE. I know you did; but girls are so queer, you never know just what they mean! They say "No" when they mean "Yes", and drive a man out of his wits for the fun of it.

JO. I don't. I never wanted to make you care for me like this, and I went away to keep you from it if I could.

LAURIE. I thought so; it was like you to do that, but it was no use. I only loved you all the more, and I worked hard at college to please you. I gave up billiards and everything you didn't like, and waited and hoped you'd love me, though I'm not half good enough—

JO. Yes, you are; you're a great deal too good for me, and I'm so grateful to you, and so proud and fond of you, I don't see why I can't love you as you want me to. I've tried, but I can't change my feelings, and it would be a lie to say I do when I don't.

LAURIE. Really, truly, Jo?

JO. Really, truly, Laurie. Oh, I'm so sorry, so desperately sorry! I wish you wouldn't take it so hard; I can't help it—you know it's impossible for people to make themselves love other people if they don't.

LAURIE. They do sometimes.

JO. I don't believe it's the right sort of love, and I'd rather not try it. (*Pause.*) Laurie, I want to tell you something.

LAURIE. Don't tell me that, Jo; I couldn't bear it now!

JO (*surprised*). Tell you what?

LAURIE. That you love that old man.

JO. What old man?

LAURIE. That devilish professor you were always writing home about. If you say you love him, I know I shall do something desperate!

JO. Don't swear, Laurie! He isn't old, nor anything bad; but good and kind, and the best friend I've got—next to you. Now don't fly into a passion! I want to be kind, but I know I shall get angry if you abuse my professor. I haven't the least idea of loving him, or anybody else.

LAURIE. But you will, after a while, and then what will become of me?

JO. What am I to do with you? Now, you haven't heard what I wanted to tell you. Sit down and listen, like a sensible boy, for I do want to do what is right and try to make you happy! I have talked this over with Mother, and I agree with her, that we are not really suited to each other. We both have quick tempers and strong wills which would probably make us very miserable if we were so foolish as to— (*She pauses slightly.*)

LAURIE. Marry? No, we shouldn't be miserable! If you love me— No, I should be a perfect saint—for you can make me anything you like!

Jo. No, I can't. I've tried it and failed, and I won't risk our happiness by such a serious experiment. Now do be reasonable, and take a sensible view of the case. You'll get over this after a while, and find some lovely, accomplished girl who will adore you, and make a much more suitable wife for you in your fine house. I shouldn't, for I am homely and awkward and odd, and you'd be ashamed of me, and we should quarrel—we can't help it even now, you see—and I shouldn't like elegant society and you would; and you'd hate my scribbling, and I couldn't get on without it, and we should be unhappy, and wish we hadn't married, and everything would be horrid!

LAURIE. Anything more?

Jo. Nothing more—except that I don't believe I shall ever marry; I'm happy as I am, and love my liberty too well to be in a hurry to give it up for any mortal man.

LAURIE. I know better! You think so now; but there'll come a time when you will care for somebody, and you'll love him tremendously, and live and die for him. I know you will, for it's your way, and I shall have to stand by and see it.

Jo. Yes, I will live and die for him, if he ever comes and makes me love him in spite of myself, and you must do the best you can! I've done all I can to help you, but you won't be reasonable, and it's selfish of you to expect me to feel just the way you want me to. I shall always be fond of you, very fond indeed, as a friend, but I'll never marry you; and the sooner you believe it, the better for both of us—so now! (*Pause.*) Let us say no more about it. We must join the others, for they will be wondering what has become of us. (*She moves to the archway and almost collides with* MR. LAURENCE, *who is about to enter the room.*)

MR. L. Why, Jo, dear! We are waiting for you and Laurie; and the coffee is getting cold.

Jo. Thank you, Mr. Laurence; we were just coming.
(*She leaves quickly.* MR. LAURENCE *lays a hand on his grandson's shoulder.*)

MR. L. I think I can guess what has happened, my boy, and I am more than sorry that things haven't worked out as you hoped. You won't care to stay at home just now, perhaps?

LAURIE. I don't intend to run away from a girl. Jo can't prevent my seeing her, and I shall stay and do it as long as I like.

MR. L. Not if you are the gentleman I think you are. I am disappointed, too, but Jo cannot help her feelings; the only thing for you to do is to go away for a time. Why not go abroad, as you planned, and forget it?

LAURIE. That wouldn't help me at all. You see, I didn't mean to go alone; Jo has always longed to travel, and I thought that, together, we might have— (*He breaks off miserably, and looks away.*)

MR. L. Now, my dear boy, I know just how you feel, for I have been through it all before, once in my own young days, and then with your father. Listen to what I have to say, for I have a plan which I think may appeal to you.

LAURIE (*without interest*). Very well, sir; what is it?

MR. L. A change of scene, and new interests will be the best thing for you at this time—though you may not think so just now. Furthermore, there is no need for you to go alone; I shall be ready and glad to go with you. There is that business in London; I meant that you should attend to it, but it would probably be better if I dealt with it myself. My partners and Brooke will look after the business here very well in my absence, so there is no reason why I should not accompany you.

LAURIE. But you hate travelling, sir; I can't ask it of you at your age.

MR. L. Bless your soul, I'm not superannuated yet! I quite enjoy the idea; it will do me good, and my old bones won't suffer, for travelling nowadays is almost as easy as sitting in a chair at home.

LAURIE. But, grandfather, we should be away for several months; you would find it—

MR. L. Let me make it clear, my boy, that I don't mean to be a burden or a hindrance to you. I go because I think you need some company to make the actual journey, but I don't intend to gad about with you, but leave you free to come and go as you choose. Italy, Germany, Switzerland—where you will—to your heart's content.

LAURIE. Just as you like, sir; it doesn't matter very much to me where I go or what I do now.

MR. L. It does to me, Laurie, remember that; and it will not be so very long before it does to you once again. You'll see, you'll see!

Together they leave the room as the lights fade.

SCENE 4

Early the following spring. It is late evening; the lamps are lit and a fire burns in the grate. When the lights rise we find MR. MARCH *and* MEG *seated in the parlour; the former is reading a book, and the latter is busy with some sewing, but it is obvious that they are ill at ease and very much preoccupied with something else. After a moment or two,* MR. MARCH *lays down his book, and stares into the fire, an expression of great sadness in his eyes; while, from time to time,* MEG *glances anxiously upstairs.* MRS. MARCH *comes downstairs. Her face is tired and drawn, and her step is heavy.*

MEG (*rising and moving quickly to her mother*). How is she, Mother?

MRS. M. She is breathing a little more quietly now, and has just dropped off to sleep. Jo and Hannah insisted on my coming down here for a rest until she wakes. I don't like leaving her, but, as she is sleeping, there is really nothing I can do, I suppose.

MR. M. Come to the fire, my dear; you look cold. (*He places a shawl around her shoulders as she seats herself.*)

MEG. Would you like a hot drink, or something to eat?

MRS. M. No, thank you, dear; I'll just sit here quietly for a while and talk to you both. I think that will help me more than anything; it is so silent upstairs, sitting with Jo and Hannah at Beth's bedside, listening only to her poor little struggling gasps for breath.

MEG. Has she spoken at all since I went up to see her?

MRS. M. No, she just lies there quiet and uncomplaining, with a tired smile for each of us whenever we do something for her. There is a strange, transparent look about her face now, as if that which is mortal is being slowly refined away—leaving the immortal to shine through the frail flesh with a pathetic beauty that is difficult to describe. Poor little Beth, she is so weak, and yet she tries so hard to be cheerful for our sakes. Oh, Arthur, I— (*Her voice breaks and she stretches out her hand in distress towards her husband.* MR. MARCH *takes it quickly and puts his other arm around her.*)

MR. M. Now, my dear, you have been wonderfully brave so far, and, by being so, have helped Beth and the rest of us more than you can know. We mustn't fail her now; it would trouble her to see your distress, for it is her greatest wish to make things easy for us; in return we must hide the pain in our hearts as best we may.

MEG. Father is right, Mother; Beth has always prayed that when the time comes for "the tide to go out", as she puts it, that it will go out easily. For her sake we must do all that we can to make it so.

MR. M. I have taken great courage and strength from Beth herself. To see her as she was some weeks ago, when pain claimed her for its own, tormented, but never forgetful of the rest of us, helped me immeasurably to face what is now past and what is yet to come. The worst is over for her, mercifully it was brief, she has a peace and tranquillity now which is beautiful to see. Let us try to take heart and comfort from that, shall we, my dear?

MRS. M. "When the time comes for the tide to turn, may it go out easily"; so it shall, please God, so it shall! (*She dries her eyes quickly on her handkerchief.*) Now, talk to me of something else, Meg; it will help me to be brighter when I go back to Beth.

MEG. Have you heard from Amy this week?

MRS. M. Oh, yes, we had a letter by yesterday's post, but I forgot to tell you. They have moved on to Switzerland, and are staying now at Vevey. I wish that Laurie was still with them, for it would be such a help and comfort for Amy to have him near when—when anything happens.

MEG. What a pity that he had to rejoin his grandfather in Paris so soon.

MR. M. Yes, it is unfortunate, but it could not be helped. Laurie had been in Nice with the Carrols and Amy for over a month, and as he had intended to stay only a week, he could not delay his return to Mr. Laurence any longer.

MEG. I fancy that when he went down to see Amy and the others at Christmastime he was tired of wandering about in Europe alone. After five months of it he must have been feeling rather homesick for familiar faces.

MRS. M. Yes, I think that is why he remained there so much longer than he intended. They certainly had some happy times together during his stay—walking, driving, having picnics, and going to balls. Amy's letters were full of their activities, and I think she has missed him very much since he left.

MEG. I wonder if he told her about Jo refusing him.

MRS. M. I think not, for I am sure that she would have mentioned it in her letters. Naturally I said nothing when writing, but left it for Jo to tell her if she so wished. But Amy is very intuitive, and I have no doubt that before Laurie left for Paris she had guessed the true state of affairs.

MEG. Poor boy, I do hope this long holiday has helped him to get over what Jo calls his "love-lornity". He was very miserable when he went away.

MR. M. I rather think it has. From one or two things he has said in his letters to us, I gain the impression that he is not finding it nearly so difficult as he had expected to forget the great love of his young life.

MEG. Well, I'm glad that Amy was able to help cheer him up, for he certainly needed it. It is a pity that she will not be able to do more, but they will be sailing for home very shortly, will they not?

MR. M. We are not sure when exactly they are making their departure. Uncle Carrol seems disinclined to leave Europe; he has already postponed the date once so that they might spend a longer time in Switzerland.

MRS. M. I fear that it will not be a very happy homecoming for Amy. I wonder if I have done right in not letting her know just how serious things are at home here? But Beth begged me to write only that she was poorly, and that it was nothing to worry about. She said that if Amy thought it was serious, she would want to come home at once, and that that would be a pity, for she should travel and see as much as she could whilst she had the chance.

MEG. That is typical of Beth; her thoughts always of others and of what is best for them—never of herself. But it is going to be a dreadful shock to Amy when she does learn the truth.

MRS. M. Yes, that is why I have written privately to Aunt and Uncle Carrol to prepare them, and, also, to Laurie. I have explained the true state of affairs, and implored him, should anything happen to Beth before they leave Europe, to go to Amy at once if he can. He is so much one of the family that it would be a great comfort for her to have him to turn to at such a time.

MEG. Oh, Mother, I am sure that he will be glad to do it. It would be a wonderful comfort for us to know that—

(MEG *breaks off suddenly, for* JO *has appeared on the stairs and is descending swiftly. As she enters the parlour the others turn expectantly towards her.*)

JO. Mother, Father, perhaps you'd better come. I think that—the tide is starting to go out.

MRS. MARCH *rises and starts to move towards the stairs; suddenly she stops and sobs as a great wave of grief passes over her.* MEG *and* JO *move quickly to her side to comfort her, and, with loving hands, lead her gently upstairs.* MR. MARCH *stares after them, and then begins to follow; near the archway he pauses, turns back, and slowly crosses the room to* BETH'S *piano. For a moment or two he stands looking at it, then very gently and lovingly, he lowers the lid over the keys. He is still standing there, his hands resting on the piano, his head bowed in silent grief, as the lights fade.*

ACT THREE

Scene I

A morning early in the following September. Beth's *photograph, with a little bow of black ribbon decorating the frame, now stands on her piano, which remains closed.*

When the lights rise Jo *is discovered busily dusting the parlour; at the piano she pauses and, taking up* Beth's *picture, looks sadly and lovingly at it for a moment or two, then carefully she replaces it, and briskly resumes her labours. As she does so* Mr. March *enters from the hall with a newspaper in his hand.*

Mr. M. No post again from Amy and Laurie; that is strange, it must be nearly a fortnight now since last we heard from them. I hope nothing is amiss.

Jo. I shouldn't think so, Father; Mr. Laurence or Aunt or Uncle Carrol would have written if anything was wrong.

Mr. M. (*seating himself*). Yes, that is so; but we have been hearing from them so regularly lately that this sudden silence seems odd. I have been expecting to hear the date of their departure, for they will be sailing for home soon, I imagine. It is a happy thought that they will all be coming back together—that is, unless Uncle Carrol has changed his mind once again, and set them all about with their arrangements at the last minute.

Jo. Oh, I hope not, for I am so looking forward to their arriving together as one big party; besides, it will make the voyage pleasanter for Mr. Laurence to have Aunt and Uncle for company, and Amy to be with—

(*During this speech* Mrs. March *has entered the parlour. She is still in mourning and is dressed for outdoors.*)

Mrs. M. I am just going over to Meg's with those jars of preserves which I promised her. Poor dear, she can make delicious jam and chutney, but the art of getting her black-currant jelly to "jell" still eludes her! Hannah and I bottled rather a lot this year, and, as John's taste for it is as marked as ever, I am taking over half a dozen jars just to keep him sweet!

Mr. M. (*from behind his paper*). Does he need that to keep him sweet, then?

Mrs. M. No, of course not, Arthur, and well you know it! I thank God daily that Meg is so happily married, and nicely settled down in her little home. There was a time—two or three months ago—when I began to wonder whether she was not in danger of damaging that happiness. She was getting so absorbed with the babies that she started neglecting everything else—including John. However, that is past now, for she has so organized herself and her domestic routine that she has time and love for them all.

Mr. M. I suppose that her mother wouldn't have had anything to do with that, by any chance?

Mrs. M. Arthur! There is no deceiving you, is there?

Mr. M. I'm afraid not, my dear; my memory is as yet, unimpaired, and I seem to remember an exactly similar state of affairs once before somewhere.

Jo. And what does all that mean, Marmee? It sounds very mysterious.

Mrs. M. Well, dear, in what was happening to Meg, I could see history repeating itself. When you and she were little, I went on in just the same way, feeling that I didn't do my duty unless I devoted myself wholly to you. Poor father took to his books, after I had refused all offers of help, and left me to try my experiment alone. I struggled along as well as I could until I fell sick; then he came to the rescue, quietly managed everything, and made himself so helpful that I saw my mistake, and never have been able to get on without him since.

Mr. M. That is the secret of our home happiness; your mother does not let domestic worries destroy her interest in my activities, and I try not to let my work make me forgetful of the little cares and duties home here that affect us all. We each do our parts, alone in many things, but at home we work always together.

Jo. Yes, of course; and you told Meg about that?

Mrs. M. I felt I had to before things went too far; poor John was being left out of everything, and Meg was rapidly becoming a slave to Daisy and Demi. As you know, I don't like interfering in any way, but I could see that trouble lay ahead for them all if something wasn't done about it. Luckily Meg made an opening for me one day by asking my opinion. She quickly saw the dangers and—well—everything's all right now!

Jo. It certainly is! Why, only yesterday I was thinking how much improved Meg is in every way since she has been married, how happy she is with John and the children, and how much they are all doing for each other. I suppose that marriage isn't such a bad thing, after all. I wonder if I should blossom out half as well as she has done, if I tried it—always providing I had the chance!

Mr. M. It's just what you need to bring out the tender, womanly half of your nature, Jo. You are like a chestnut burr, prickly outside, but silky soft within.

Mrs. M. Love will make you show your heart some day, my dear, and then the rough burr will fall off.

Jo. Well, frost opens chestnut burrs, Mother, and it takes a good shake to bring them down.

(HANNAH *appears from the kitchen bringing the jars of preserves in a basket covered with a cloth.*)

HANNAH. Here's the preserves, mum, and I've made a special egg custard which I've put in for the bairns. They're only babbies yet, but they've a real partiality for it already, and it's full of goodness.

MRS. M. Thank you, Hannah. I can see that if Meg doesn't succeed in spoiling those twins you will!
HANNAH. Well if they're not spoilt a bit now, I'd like to know when they're going to be! Have you nearly finished the dusting, Miss Jo? I was just coming in to do the brass. If I'm not careful, I shall be getting all behind with my work. (*She goes off.*)
MR. M. There speaks the voice of wisdom! And if I'm not careful, I shall be getting all behind with my work, too. I really must get back to my study. Good-bye, my dear, give my love to Meg and the babies. I'll leave you to your dusting, Jo. (*He goes upstairs.*)
JO (*as she resumes her dusting*). Marmee, did you really mean that—about love making me show my heart some day?
MRS. M. Why, yes, dear, of course. What makes you ask?
JO. Oh, I don't know. I've never really thought much about it, before; but, lately, ever since Amy became engaged to Laurie, I've wondered—
MRS. M. You mean that with Meg married, poor Beth gone, and now Amy engaged, you're wondering if you've been left on the shelf?
JO. Well, it does rather look as though I'm going to be an old maid. A literary spinster, with a pen for a spouse, a family of stories for children, and twenty years hence, perhaps, if I'm lucky, a morsel of fame—when I'm too old to enjoy it. Oh, I dare say old maids are very comfortable when they get used to it, but—
MRS. M. Oh, Jo! I don't think I should worry about that too soon if I were you!
JO. Well, perhaps not. Oh, dear, I am sorry for myself, aren't I? Tell me, Mother—I've been wanting to ask you—are you really happy about Amy and Laurie being engaged?
MRS. M. Yes, more than happy. I hoped it would come to pass, for I am very fond of that young man, and they will make ideal partners for each other, I am sure. I was not entirely surprised, for I had sensed a subtle change in her from the way she wrote, and I traced it back to about the time that Laurie arrived in Nice last Christmas. There was a hint here and there in her letters, of which I am sure she was quite unconscious, that made me suspect that love and Laurie would win the day.
JO. How sharp you were, Marmee, and how silent! You never said a word to me.
MRS. M. Mothers have need of sharp eyes and discreet tongues, when they have girls to manage. But it was not so very difficult to foresee; when Laurie went to her in Switzerland after we lost Beth, Amy turned to him in grief, and found not only comfort, but abiding love which she then realized she returned. Sad at heart as we were here, I could guess what would happen. I was half afraid to put the idea into your head, lest you should write and congratulate them before the thing was settled.

Jo. I'm not the scatterbrain I was; you may trust me, for I am sober and sensible enough to be anyone's confidante now.

Mrs. M. So you are, dear, and I should have made you mine, only I fancied it might pain you to learn that your Laurie loved anyone else.

Jo. Now, Mother, did you really think I could be so silly and selfish after I had refused his love?

Mrs. M. I knew you were sincere then, Jo; but lately I have thought that if he came back, and asked again, you might, perhaps, feel like giving another answer. Forgive me, dear, I can't help seeing that you are very lonely, and sometimes there is a look in your eyes that goes to my heart; so I fancied that Laurie might fill the empty place, if he tried now.

Jo. No, Mother, it is better as it is, and I'm glad that Amy has learned to love him. But you are right in one thing; I am lonely and perhaps if Laurie had tried again, I might have said "Yes", not because I love him any more, but because I care more to be loved than when he went away.

Mrs. M. I am glad of that, Jo, for it shows that you are getting on.

Jo. It's very curious, but the more I try to satisfy myself with all sorts of natural affection, the more I seem to want. I'd no idea that hearts could take in so many—mine is so elastic, it never seems full now, and I used to be quite contented with my family; I don't understand it.

Mrs. M. I do.

Jo. Do you remember that line in Amy's last letter? "It is beautiful to be loved as Laurie loves me; I see and feel it in all he says and does, and it makes me so happy and so humble that I don't seem to be the same girl I was." And that's our cool, reserved, and worldly Amy! Truly love does work miracles—so there must be something in it, after all!

Mrs. M. Well, it's been responsible for some remarkable transformations before now! But not only love will have changed our Amy. It is over two years since we saw her and she will have grown into a young woman with all the polish and assurance that foreign travel imparts. We shall hardly know her when she comes home.

(HANNAH *enters.*)

HANNAH. Are you not gone yet, mum? You'll have no time with Miss Meg and the children before you have to come back for lunch if you don't go soon.

Mrs. M. Good gracious, yes! Jo and I have been gossiping, and I hadn't noticed the time. Good-bye, Jo dear, don't worry too much—things will come right for you, perhaps when you least expect it. Good-bye, Hannah. I don't suppose I shall be more than about an hour.

(MRS. MARCH *goes to the front door;* HANNAH *starts to polish the brasswork in the grate.*)

Jo (*after a pause*). Hannah.

HANNAH. Yes, Miss Jo.

Jo. Do you remember, when I was a little girl, how I used to confess things to you when I was ashamed of something I had said or done?

HANNAH. Yes, you never could bear to have things on your conscience for long.

Jo. Well, I've something on my conscience now. Confession is good for the soul, I know, but I cannot say what is in my heart to either Mother or Father, for I fear it would hurt them dreadfully; so may I tell it to you?

HANNAH. Why, of course, my lamb; you tell old Hannah what's troubling your heart and we'll see if we can't put it right.

Jo. I hope you won't think any the worse of me when you know, for I do feel so terribly mean having such thoughts; but it must be said or I shall burst! You see, before Beth died I promised her that I would do my best to take her place and help Mother and Father to get over their grief.

HANNAH. And so you have, love; you're a thoughtful creature, and you've done your best for us all, so that we shouldn't miss that dear one more than you could help. Your Ma and Pa may not say much, but they see it, and it's a great comfort and consolation to them, you may be sure.

Jo. I'm glad you think so, Hannah. But, though I try hard, my spirit rebels so; it's not that I don't want to do all I can for Mother and Father—I love them too much to want to do otherwise. I suppose if I was the heroine of a moral story-book I should have become quite saintly, renounced the world, and gone about doing good in a mortified bonnet and with a pocketful of tracts. But I'm not a heroine, and, now, as time is going on, I begin to feel something very like despair at the thought of spending all my life here, devoted to humdrum cares, and duty that never seems to grow any easier. I can't do it; I wasn't meant for a life like this, and I know I shall break away and do something desperate if somebody doesn't come to help me.

HANNAH. Now, now, my pet; don't take on so. Your own grief at losing Miss Beth—which you've rarely shown—is half to blame for this. You've been that busy trying to make the house cheerful, that your own heart has had to smother its feelings—and that is something you can only do for so long. You need something fresh to occupy your mind. Why don't you try writing your stories again? That always used to make you happy.

Jo. Mother suggested that, too, but I've no heart to write; and if I had, none of the publishers or editors seem to care for my work.

HANNAH. Well, we do; write something for us, Miss Jo, and never mind the rest of the world. Try it, now; I'm sure it would do you good, and give us pleasure, too.

Jo. I don't know if I can, but—well—I'll try.

HANNAH. That's the idea! We can't have you in the doldrums! You're the one that always keeps the rest of us going! Land sakes! I must go to the kitchen; I've a cake in the oven and I don't want it to burn.

Jo. I'll finish the brass for you, Hannah.

HANNAH. Bless you, that will be a help.

Jo. Thank you for hearing my confessions; you don't think too badly of me for what I said?

HANNAH. If you've nothing worse than that to tell me ever, you'll not go far wrong!

(HANNAH *goes to her kitchen.* JO *sets to work on the fender.* LAURIE *moves quietly into the archway from the direction of the front door. He is looking a little older and has grown a small moustache. He stands looking around the room with all the pleasure of recognition and at the back of the figure at the fireplace with special affection. Suddenly he moves forward quietly, and puts his hands in front of* JO's *eyes.*)

LAURIE. Guess who!

(JO *gives a little cry of surprise, and then pulling his hands away from her eyes, she turns joyfully to* LAURIE.)

Jo. Laurie! Oh, my dear Laurie! What a surprise!

LAURIE. Dear Jo, are you glad to see me then?

Jo. Glad! Oh, words can't express my gladness! But you're alone! Where's Amy?

LAURIE. Your mother has got her, down at Meg's. We stopped there on our way up, and there was no getting my wife out of their clutches.

Jo. Your what?

LAURIE. Oh, the dickens, now I've done it!

Jo. You've gone and got married?

LAURIE. Yes, please, but I never will again. (*He drops on his knees with a penitent clasping of hands that is not entirely convincing.*)

Jo. Actually married?

LAURIE. Very much so, thank you.

Jo. Mercy on us! What dreadful thing will you do next?

LAURIE. A characteristic, but not exactly complimentary congratulation.

Jo. What can you expect when you take one's breath away, creeping in like a burglar, and letting cats out of bags like that? Get up, you ridiculous boy, and tell me all about it.

LAURIE. Not until you tell me how I look. Haven't I the appearance of a married man, and the head of a family?

Jo. Not in the least, and you never will. You've grown bigger and bonnier, and I like your moustache—it suits you—but you are the same scapegrace as ever. How is Amy looking? I cannot wait to see her.

LAURIE. She'll be here in a moment; they were following on behind me. But I couldn't wait; I wanted to be the one to tell you the grand surprise, and have "first skim" as we used to say when we squabbled about the cream.

Jo. Of course you did, and then spoilt your story by beginning at the wrong end. Now, start right, and tell me how it all happened, for I'm longing to know.

LAURIE. You must wait a little—I must leave some of the story for Amy to tell—especially as I've had all the fun of breaking the news to you! But, before she comes, Jo, dear, I want to say one thing, and then we'll put it by for ever. As I told you in my letter, when I wrote that Amy and I were getting engaged, I never shall stop loving you; but the love is altered, and I have learned to see that it is better as it is. Amy and you change places in my heart, that's all. I think it was meant to be so, and would have come about naturally, if I had waited, as you tried to make me; but I never could be patient, and so I got a heartache. Upon my word, I was so tumbled up in my mind at one time that I didn't know which I loved best—you or Amy, and tried to love you both alike! But when I saw her in Switzerland everything seemed to clear up all at once. You both got into your right places, and I felt sure that it was well off with the old love, before it was on with the new. Do you understand what I mean, Jo? Can we go back to the happy old times, and the same relationship we had, when we first knew one another?

Jo. I understand what you mean, with all my heart; but, Laurie, we never can be boy and girl again—those happy old times can't come back, and we mustn't expect it. We are man and woman now; I am sure that you feel this as I do, for I see the change in you, and you'll find it in me. I shall miss the boy, but I shall love and admire the man more, because he means to be what I hoped he would.

(*Before* LAURIE *can reply there is the sound of the front door opening and excited voices in the hall.* AMY *is heard calling* "Jo! Jo! Where is she? Where's my dear old Jo?" *A moment later she appears in the archway with* MRS. MARCH *behind her. She has grown into a poised and mature woman, and is very fashionably dressed. With cries of delight the sisters throw themselves at each other.*)

Amy! My dear, dear girl! How lovely to see you again!

AMY. Oh, Jo, Jo! I can hardly believe that I am truly home! It's been so long away from you all!

Jo. How elegant you look! And so grown up! Doesn't she, Marmee?

MRS. M. Yes, for a moment I hardly knew who this grand lady was when she opened the door to me at Meg's! Now I must go and fetch Hannah! (*She goes to the kitchen.*)

AMY. I suppose Laurie has told you our great surprise? He wanted so much to be the first to tell you.

Jo. Yes, but he hasn't explained how it all came about—he said he would leave that for you! Now, you must sit down and tell me everything. But—wait a moment—where's Mr. Laurence? Isn't he with you?

LAURIE. Oh, yes, of course; but he was so tired after the journey that he begged to be excused and drove straight home after dropping us at Meg's. He's going to call to see you this evening.

(MRS. MARCH *reappears with* HANNAH, *who is in a state of great excitement.*)

HANNAH. Land sakes, Miss Amy, is it really you? Blest if she ain't in silk from head to foot, and looking that genteel! Welcome home, my pet! Ain't it a relishing sight to see you! And you, too, Mr. Laurie! Bless me, if the whole place ain't been that silent without you and your noisy pranks! It'll be good to have you back—even though I shan't know what's going to happen next!

JO. Now, everyone, do let's settle down, so that we may hear all about this wonderful wedding and how it came to pass. (*There is a general movement as everyone finds a seat.*) Laurie, you start—for I can't wait any longer.

LAURIE. Well, I did it to please Amy!

JO. Fib number one; Amy did it to please you. Isn't that right, Amy?

AMY. Quite right! It really came about in this way; as you know, we were all coming home together this month, but suddenly Uncle Carrol changed his mind once again—he is the most erratic man—and decided that he would like to pass another winter in Paris.

LAURIE. But Grandpa didn't wish to stay any longer, and, as he went to please me, I couldn't let him make the return journey alone—neither could I leave Amy. Unfortunately, Mrs. Carrol had got a lot of English notions about chaperons and such nonsense, and wouldn't let Amy come with us. So I just settled the difficulty by saying: "Let's be married, and then we can do as we like."

JO. Of course you did; you always have things to suit you.

LAURIE. Not always.

MRS. M. How did you ever get Aunt Carrol to agree?

AMY. It was hard work; but between us we talked her over, for we had heaps of good reasons on our side. There wasn't time to write and ask leave, Mother, but you and Father had consented to our engagement so we thought that it was only "taking time by the fetlock" as Jo used to say.

JO. But when and where did this great occasion take place?

AMY. Three weeks ago at the American consul's in Paris—a very quiet wedding, of course, for even in our happiness we didn't forget dear little Beth.

MRS. M. But why didn't you let us know afterwards?

AMY. We wanted to surprise you all, and, as we were coming directly home, we thought we should be here almost as soon as a letter, and would be able to share the fun and rejoicing with you.

Jo. Well, I just can't make it true that you children are really married, and going to set up housekeeping! Why, it seems only yesterday that I was buttoning Amy's pinafore, and pulling Laurie's hair when he teased. Mercy me, how time does fly!

LAURIE. As one of the children is older than yourself, you needn't talk quite so much like a grandma. I flatter myself that I'm a "gentleman growed".

Jo. You may be a little older in years, but I'm ever so much older in feeling, Laurie. Women always are! I was just wondering how you two get on together.

LAURIE. Like angels!

Jo. Yes, of course, at first—but who rules?

LAURIE. I don't mind telling you that Amy does, now; at least I let her think so—it pleases her, you know.

Jo. You'll go on as you begin, and Amy will rule you all the days of your life. That ever I should live to see you a henpecked husband and enjoying it! Well, if she abuses you, come to me and I'll defend you!

AMY. Oh, Jo! You haven't changed! I ask you, does he look as though he needs defending? But you must certainly check me if I do start "hen-pecking"!

Jo. Oh, you'll get on all right together; you never used to quarrel with Laurie as I did when we were younger—so there's no reason to suppose that you'll start now!

MRS. M. What are you going to do with yourselves after you get settled?

LAURIE. Oh, we have great plans; we don't mean to say much about them yet, because we are such very new brooms, but we don't intend to be idle. I'm going into business with a devotion that shall delight grandpa, and prove to him that all these months dawdling about in Europe have not spoilt me.

MRS. M. And, Amy, my dear, what of you?

LAURIE. After doing the civil all around, and airing our best bonnet, we shall astonish you by the elegant hospitalities of our mansion, the brilliant society we shall draw about us, and the beneficial influence we shall exert over the world at large. That's about it, isn't it, Madame Récamier?

AMY. Time will show, Mr. Impertinence; and don't shock my family by calling me names before their faces! I have every intention of creating a home with a good wife in it, before I set up a *salon* as a queen of Society!

MRS. M. Goodness me! We've been so busy chattering that we've forgotten all about poor Father! He's upstairs in his study. We must go to him at once.

AMY. Oh, Mother, is he at home? I thought he must be out visiting or at a meeting. Do let's creep up and surprise him!

LAURIE. That's a marvellous idea! Come on, Madam Mother, you go up first and tell him that a young married couple have called to see him, and then we'll burst in on him.

MRS. M. Poor man, little does he know what is coming to him! Now, not too much noise as we go up or he'll suspect we're playing a joke—he's too used to Jo's pranks.

(*With many suppressed laughs and giggles, cries of* "Ssh!" *and general merriment* MRS. MARCH, AMY *and* LAURIE *go upstairs.*)

HANNAH. Don't they look as fine as two fiddles? Fancy our little Miss Amy being a married woman; and "Mrs. Laurence", no less!

JO. Yes, it is rather wonderful, isn't it?

HANNAH. I suppose she'll be riding in her own carriage now, and using all them lovely silver dishes over yonder at the big house?

JO. Shouldn't wonder if she drove six white horses, ate off gold plate, and wore diamonds and point-lace every single day. I'm sure that Laurie thinks nothing is too good for her! (*She goes upstairs after the others.*)

HANNAH. No more there is! Will you have hash or fish-balls for lunch?

JO (*off*). I really don't care!

(HANNAH, *chuckling delightedly, starts for the kitchen, but is arrested by a sudden ring at the front-door bell. She crosses to the front door, and shortly reappears with a thick-set, bearded gentleman who looks nervously around the room and plucks at his hat and gloves.*)

HANNAH. Please do wait here and take a seat a moment, sir; I'll tell Miss Jo. (*She moves to the stairs and calls.*) Miss Jo. There's a gentleman here to see you! (*She turns back, and before disappearing into her kitchen reassures the visitor.*) She'll not be a minute, sir; we've just got some very unexpected company!

(*From above there comes the sound of laughter and voices raised in delighted surprise. Left to himself, the bearded gentleman listens nervously and then rises as though he would leave as suddenly as he arrived. However, before he can do so* JO *quickly descends the stairs and enters the parlour. As soon as she sees him she comes to an abrupt halt, a mixture of absolute amazement and pure delight in her face.*)

JO. Mr. Bhaer! Of all people! (*She moves quickly to him and shakes his hand warmly.*) What a day this is! Oh, Mr. Bhaer, I am so glad to see you!

MR. B. And I to see you, Miss Marsch. (*From above comes a further outburst of laughter. He looks upwards as he hears it, and makes a move as if to go.*) But you haf a party; it is not polite that I stay now.

JO (*making a gesture to detain him*). No, not a party—only the family. My sister has just come home from abroad. Do you remember my telling you about Amy, who was in Europe? Well, she arrived just a short time ago. Oh, you must stay and meet everyone. Do sit down, please.

MR. B. If I shall not be Monsieur de Trop I will so gladly make their acquaintances. (*He pauses, and looks more closely at* Jo.) You haf been ill, my friend? You do not look so well as when last I see you.

Jo. Not ill, but tired and rather sorrowful; we have had a great sadness here since I came home from New York.

MR. B. Ah, yes, I know; my heart was sore for you when I hear of that from Mrs. Kirke. But you haf brightness in the house again now, eh?

Jo. Oh, yes! More than you know, for Amy has not only arrived home unexpectedly, but has surprised us all by bringing a husband home, too!

MR. B. So? And you, Miss Marsch, you haf not found a husband yet?

Jo. Me? Goodness, no! Whatever makes you ask?

MR. B. Forgif me, but when you were in New York you speak often of a young neighbour called "Lowree"—of whom you seem to have the great regard. I thought, perhaps—

Jo (*with a laugh*). Mercy me, no! You had quite the wrong impression. But, of course, you don't know! You see, Laurie has been in Europe since I came home, and now he is the husband that Amy has brought back with her!

MR. B. (*after a slight pause*). So? I am glad for them, so very glad.

Jo (*changing the subject*). Well, this is a lovely surprise! Quite a red-letter day for me! But what brings you to this part of the world?

MR. B. I haf a little business in the city which keeps me here for a few days, so I think I go to see my old friend Miss Marsch, who so kindly ask me to call if ever I come this way.

Jo. But, of course! I should have been very cross if you hadn't come to see me.

(MRS. MARCH, *who has descended the stairs during this dialogue, now enters the parlour.*)

Oh, Mother, this is my friend, Professor Bhaer; he's called to see us as he promised he would. Mr. Bhaer, this is my mother.

MRS. M. (*shaking hands*). How do you do, Professor Bhaer; I feel I know you quite well, for Jo wrote and told us a great deal about you whilst she was in New York.

MR. B. Thank you; that is kind, Mrs. Marsch. I, too, haf heard much about you.

MRS. M. It is nice of you to call to see us. Won't you stay to lunch? We are just welcoming our daughter and new son-in-law from abroad, and you would be most welcome to join us.

MR. B. No, dear madam, I thank you; but it would not be polite for me to intrude. Such an occasion is for the family alone. I call only to pay my respects. But, if you will gif me leave, I shall come again.

(MRS. MARCH *moves to the mantelpiece and rings a small handbell to summon* HANNAH.)

Mrs. M. But, of course, please do! We shall be delighted to see you. Will you take tea with us tomorrow afternoon?
Mr. B. I should be most honoured.
Mrs. B. About four o'clock—if that is convenient?
Mr. B. I shall look forward to it. Until then, *auf wiedersehen*, madam. (*He takes the hand which* Mrs. March *offers, and shakes it, accompanying the action with a little formal bow.*)
Mrs. M. Good-bye until tomorrow, Mr. Bhaer. I am very glad to have met you; please remember that there is always a welcome waiting for you in this house.
Mr. B. I thank you. *Auf wiedersehen*, Miss Marsch; it gifs me much pleasure to meet with you again.
Jo. Good-bye, Mr. Bhaer; I look forward to a long gossip with you tomorrow.
(*With a further bow for each lady,* Mr. Bhaer *turns to* Hannah, *who has, meantime, appeared in the hall, and is conducted to the front door.* Jo *moves to the window to peer out at him as he makes his departure.*)
Mrs. M. What a very thoughtful and understanding man, Jo. It will be a pleasure to get to know him better.
Jo. Yes, I thought you'd like him. (*She turns from the window, her face glowing—all traces of her former depression now completely dispelled; suddenly she chuckles—she is quite her old self—as she moves back into the room.*) But, dear old fellow, I've never seen him looking so neat and tidy! He couldn't have got himself up with more care if he'd been going a-wooing!
A sudden thought occurs to her, and she comes to an abrupt stop, her hand at her mouth. Mrs. March *smiles quietly to herself, but says nothing, as the lights fade.*

Scene 2

About a fortnight later. It is a dull, wet autumn afternoon, and the lights rise to disclose a fire burning brightly in the grate; Mr. March *standing, book in hand, before the bookshelves; and* John Brooke *seated quietly near by. The older man is busy expounding his views on education, a subject dear to his heart.*

Mr. M. There is no doubt about it, the education of the young is both a challenge and a sacred trust. The taking of fresh, young minds, and guiding them into the ways of clear thinking and sound reasoning, as a preparation for life, is one of the most deeply satisfying occupations I know.
John. I agree with you, sir, and the thought is very much before me when I think of the two young minds in my own home—which daily become more of a responsibility.

Mr. M. Yes, Daisy and Demi will soon be keeping us busy with questions on every conceivable topic. I don't think that one can start preparing them too soon; a good foundation is most necessary for all later knowledge. To my mind, many of our ideas on teaching are decidedly unimaginative and stagnant. I have thought for some time that the Socratic method of education has much to commend it, and that it might be more generally used in this country.

JOHN (*with a laugh*). Quite possibly, sir; but I feel it would be a rather involved method to adopt for teaching the twins their alphabet!

MR. M. (*also laughing*). Yes, John, I think you may be right there! But, even with such elementary instruction, there is no reason why the task should not be made as pleasant and enjoyable as possible; with the very young, like the twins, it is all-important to capture the imagination. (*Warming to his theme.*) Lessons should never be associated with dullness and boredom. Now, I have evolved a system for teaching the alphabet which, with your permission, I should like to try out on Daisy and Demi.

JOHN. Why, certainly; but exactly what form does it take?

MR. M. I am convinced that it is important for the minds and bodies of the young to work together. If a child is encouraged, therefore, to form the shape of the letter he is being taught with his arms and legs, it will make a quicker and deeper impression on his mind than any amount of drawing it out on paper.

JOHN. I don't know that I quite follow you, air.

MR. M. (*stretching his arms out on either side of him*). Well, for example, this would be "T" (*Adjusting his arms to the shape of each letter.*)—and this is "F"; and this is "P", and so on.

JOHN. Oh, I see what you mean; yes, I think that's a very good idea, but is it possible to form all the letters of the alphabet in this way?

MR. M. Not in a standing position, of course, but that wouldn't worry the twins, for they love to roll on the floor! (*He sits himself carefully on the floor in front of the sofa to continue his demonstration.*) You see, it is even easier when one can use both legs! Here we have "C" and then "I"—

JOHN (*the idea suddenly taking his fancy*). Yes, of course! The twins would find this fascinating, I'm sure! (*Trying to form the letter in a standing position.*) I suppose this would be "K"?

MR. M. That's right! But the one Demi would like in particular, I fancy, is "V"!

(*He lies back and puts his legs up to form the letter "V". Unnoticed during this discussion the door bell has sounded;* HANNAH *has crossed from the kitchen to the front door to answer it; and, just as both* MR. MARCH *and* JOHN *are most completely absorbed in their letter forming,* AUNT MARCH *appears in the archway. The first thing to meet her disapproving eye is the vision of* MR. MARCH's *feet and legs appearing above the sofa; from this it passes to observe* JOHN *doubled up in his attempt to form the letter "K". At first neither gentleman is aware of her entrance, and she has inspected both, icily, through her quizzing-glass before they become conscious of her presence in the parlour. With a measure of embarrassment they quickly assume a more normal posture. There is a further pause before* AUNT MARCH *can recover from her astonishment to speak.* HANNAH, *having viewed the remarkable scene over* AUNT MARCH'S *shoulder, has returned, somewhat perplexed, to the saner privacy of her kitchen.*)

AUNT M. Well, upon my word, Arthur! I thought that you had outgrown rolling on the floor more than half a century ago! Are you feeling quite well, or is this some form of Swedish gymnastic? And you, Mr. Brooke, from your appearance on my entrance I gained the impression that you had eaten something which had disagreed with you. Have you a pain in the abdomen, sir?

MR. M. (*slightly confused*). We are quite all right, thank you, Aunt March; I was just demonstrating a new method which I have evolved to teach the twins their alphabet.

AUNT M. If you were not a minister of the church, Arthur, and my nephew into the bargain, I should be obliged to doubt either your truthfulness or your sanity. I can only say that I thank providence that I learnt my alphabet in a more conventional manner! If my great-great-nephew and niece are to commence their education in such an indecorous and abandoned manner, I dare not think to what excesses you may lead them when they reach more advanced subjects. However, that is more than enough of that! I am here on a matter of the greatest importance, and, if you have quite finished writhing on the floor like a cat with convulsions, I should be grateful for your attention. Now, where is Margaret?

MR. M. I think she is upstairs with Meg; there was some talk of seeing a new bonnet, I believe.

AUNT M. Bonnet! This is no time to be gossiping about bonnets—new or otherwise! Mr. Brooke, be good enough to fetch my niece here at once; she may resume her fashion notes with your wife at some other time. (JOHN *goes swiftly upstairs.*) Now, Arthur, I want to know exactly what has been going on in this house during the last fortnight.

Mr. M. "Going on", Aunt March?

AUNT M. Yes, "going on"! After what I have just witnessed my worst fears begin to be realized. How you can placidly indulge in these indoor cavortments whilst your own daughter is busily going about the town making herself a subject for gossip is quite incomprehensible to me.

MR. M. A subject for gossip?

AUNT M. (*with irritation*). Oh, really, Arthur, pull yourself together! Don't stand there repeating everything I say like a parrot! I have a bird at home which makes more intelligent conversation!

MR. M. Really, Aunt March, I have no idea to what you refer.

(MRS. MARCH *who, during this dialogue, has descended the stairs, now enters the parlour with* MEG *and* JOHN *close behind her.*)

AUNT. M. Ah, Margaret! Come in, come in! Perhaps you can be a little more intelligent than your husband here!

MRS. M. (*with a look of inquiry at her husband*). Why, Aunt March, whatever is wrong? I thought you said that you would call tomorrow. We didn't expect you today.

AUNT M. (*glancing significantly at both* MR. MARCH *and* JOHN). That was quite apparent when I entered this room. I have come because I wish to discover the exact relationship that exists between Josephine and this German school-teacher whom you seem to be harbouring indefinitely.

MRS. M. "Relationship", Aunt March?

AUNT M. Now, don't you start, Margaret! I have just had Arthur repeating my every word like a mountain echo. This—this—foreign man has been here over a fortnight, has he not?

MRS. M. Not exactly here, Aunt March; he is staying in the city, but he has called to see us nearly every day.

AUNT M. Ah! That is significant in itself!

MR. M. Significant only of our esteem for him. He is an interesting and educated man, whose company we all enjoy. He was a good friend to Jo whilst she was in New York, and, by our hospitality, we are endeavouring to repay a little of that debt.

AUNT M. That's as may be! But a man who calls every day for a fortnight at a house where there is an unmarried daughter may be regarded as something more than a casual visitor fulfilling his social obligations. What goes on in this house is—mercifully—none of my business, but when I witness a niece of mine acting without due propriety in public, I feel that—

MRS. M. What do you mean, Aunt March? Please make yourself clear.

AUNT M. This very afternoon—not a quarter of an hour ago—I was driving to take tea with Mrs. Chester; as I turned into the main street I saw, with my own eyes, Josephine and this bearded, intellectual wonder—apparently in the highest spirits—walking arm-in-arm under the same umbrella! (*She pauses briefly for dramatic effect.*) Of course, I ordered the coachman to turn the carriage at once, and drove straight here.

MRS. M. (*so relieved that she cannot stifle a little laugh*). Oh, is that all!

AUNT M. Is that all! Mercy on us, to my way of thinking it is more than enough! I do not subscribe to these modern trends in behaviour. Young people, nowadays, have far too much freedom; in my young day we knew how to behave with restraint and refinement. However, I demand to know, is there some understanding between these two? Has this man asked if he might pay his addresses to Josephine? Has he given an indication of his feelings towards her?

Mr. M. Well, Aunt March, nothing has actually been said, but we rather gain the impression that Mr. Bhaer intends to marry our Jo.

Mrs. M. And I believe that she will not hesitate to accept him, for she has been happier and more contented in these last two weeks than I have known her for many years. She sings constantly about the house, does her hair up three times a day, and has become so blooming that you would hardly know her!

Meg. She has also taken to walking far more than she used to; and it is surprising how frequently hers and Mr. Bhaer's paths cross!

Aunt M. So she, at any rate, has confessed her feelings for him?

Mrs. M. Gracious, no! After a lifetime of roundly denouncing "lovering", as she calls it, Jo is finding it more than difficult to admit to being caught up in it herself, and is mortally afraid of being laughed at for being so ready to forget her declarations of independence.

Meg. None of us have dared to mention it. We have all tried to appear as though we were stone-blind to the change in Jo, and what is so obviously going on in her heart. Even Laurie—and he is her special dread—has managed to keep his peace and not tease her about it—thanks to Amy's watchfulness!

Aunt M. (*to* Mrs. March). And what do you and Arthur think of such a union?

Mr. M. Mr. Bhaer is, admittedly, rather older than Jo—and is, also, of another nationality. But we believe that Jo has sufficient strength of character and general resourcefulness to meet any problems which may arise from such differences.

Aunt M. Allowing that that may be so—though I have my doubts—his position and prospects leave much to be desired, do they not?

Mrs. M. Certainly he is not wealthy; nor does there seem to be any prospect of his ever being so. But his life has been enriched in many other ways, and he is well fitted to pursue his vocation of teaching. He is kind and thoughtful, and seems always to have Jo's interests and welfare at heart, for he can never do enough for her. If they truly love one another, then I shall raise no objection to their marrying.

Aunt M. Well, upon my word! You seem to have settled it all very nicely between you, I must say, though I do not understand why I was not consulted in the matter. I have quite despaired of Jo ever making a really suitable match with someone of wealth and position, so I suppose I must resign myself to this far from satisfactory alliance. Well, I must go, for I am already very late at Mrs. Chester's. I think, Arthur, that you should speak to this Mr. . . . Mr. . . .

Mr M. Bhaer—Mr. Bhaer.

Aunt M. Heathen name, if ever I heard one! You should speak to him at once; you may not consider that waltzing about in the streets arm-in-arm lacks propriety, but I should be at a loss to explain such behaviour to Mrs. Chester, I can assure you.

Mr. M. I do not think it will be so very long before Mr. Bhaer makes a declaration for himself without any prompting from me, Aunt March.

Aunt M. I should hope not, indeed; but foreigners have some very strange ideas in these matters.

Mrs. M. We will come with you so far as the carriage, for we are going back with Meg and John to see the babies.

Aunt M. (*pausing as she turns to go*). I should like to see Josephine married and settled down; now that Amy has a husband it is only proper that her elder sister should be in the same state. But why she could not find someone with at least a more respectable-sounding name is quite beyond me. Mrs. Bhaer—it sounds like something out of a menagerie! (*An expression of the greatest distaste on her face,* Aunt March *turns and goes out, followed by the others. A few moments pass, and then* Jo *appears cautiously from the kitchen, leading* Mr. Bhaer.)

Jo (*peering into the parlour*). Oh, good! They've gone! Come in, Mr. Bhaer. I'm sorry to have to bring you through the kitchen door, but when I saw Aunt March's carriage outside I knew it was the only way to avoid her.

Mr. B. You haf not the liking for your aunt?

Jo. Oh, she's all right, really, but she is such a dragon! Always disapproving about something or somebody, and she's always so rude to our friends that, now, I make a point of never introducing her to anyone. I can't think what she wanted here today, for she wasn't expected until tomorrow. Now, you'll have some tea, won't you?

Mr. B. One minute, Miss Marsch. I haf something to tell you which is sad for me. I did not wish to spoil our walk this afternoon, so I say nothing until now.

Jo. What is it, Mr. Bhaer?

Mr. B. I must soon be going away; my business here is done.

Jo. Successfully, I hope?

Mr. B. I ought to think so, for my friends find for me a place in a college where I teach as at home in Germany. For this I should be grateful, should I not?

Jo. Indeed, you should! How much more interesting it will be for you to teach in a college after so long with private pupils. You must come to see us often; Mother and Father are always—

Mr. B. Ah! But we shall not meet often, I fear; this place is at the West.

Jo (*disappointment in her voice*). So far away! (*For a moment she is silent.*) How soon will it be before you have to go?

Mr. B. A week, perhaps, two. My heart will be sad to leave. Miss Marsch, there is something I was going to ask of you.

Jo. Yes, sir?

Mr. B. I am bold to say it because so short a time remains to me.

Jo. Yes, sir.

MR. B. Your mother has been so very kind to me during my stay here, I wish for to gif her a little present. I thought perhaps a warm shawl would be a friendly thing to gif. Will you kindly gif me a word of taste and help when I go to buy it?

Jo (*her disappointment mounting, and tears starting in her eyes*). I'll do it with pleasure, Mr. Bhaer.

MR. B. (*suddenly becoming aware of the tears*). Heart's dearest, why do you cry?

Jo. Because you are going away.

MR. B. (*relief breaking over him*). Ah, my Gott, that is so good! Jo, I haf nothing but much love to gif you; I came to see if you could care for it, and I waited to be sure that I was something more than a friend. Am I? Can you make a little place in your heart for me?

Jo. Oh, yes! But, Friedrich, why didn't you—

MR. B. Ah! She gifs me my name!

Jo. I always call you so to myself—I forgot; but I won't unless you like it.

MR. B. Like it! It is more sweet to me than I can tell. Say "thou" also, and I shall say your language is almost as beautiful as mine.

Jo. Isn't "thou" a little sentimental?

MR. B. Sentimental? Yes; thank Gott, we Germans believe in sentiment, and keep ourselves young mit it. Your English "you" is so cold—say "thou", please, it means so much to me.

Jo (*after a slight pause*). Well, then, why didn't thou tell me all this sooner?

MR. B. Now I will tell all my heart. I had a wish to say something the day I said good-bye in New York; but I thought Lowree was betrothed to thee, and so I spoke not. Wouldst thou haf said "Yes" then, if I had spoken?

Jo. I don't know; I'm afraid not, for I didn't have any heart just then.

MR. B. Prut! that I do not believe. It was asleep till the fairy prince came through the wood and waked it up. Ah well, *"Die erste Liebe ist die beste"*; but that I should not expect.

Jo. *"Die erste Liebe ist die beste"*; yes, the first love is the best; so be contented, for I never had another. Laurie was only a boy, and soon got over his fancy.

MR. B. Good! Then I am most happy, for thou givest me all I haf waited for so long. I am grown selfish, as thou wilt find, Professorin.

Jo. "Professorin"; I like that! Now, tell me what brought you just when I most needed you?

MR. B. (*producing a newspaper cutting*). This little poem which I find one day by chance in a newspaper. I see your name as the writer, and, then, when I read I find it is about yourself and your sisters.

Jo. But how could that bring you?

MR. B. Read close and you will see. (*He passes the cutting to her and points at one verse in particular.*) There is one little verse that seemed to call me—there—this one.

Jo (*reading*). "Hints of a woman early old;
　　　　　　A woman in a lonely home,
　　　　　　Hearing like a sad refrain—
　　　　　'Be worthy love, and love will come,
　　　　　　In the falling summer rain.'"

It's very bad poetry, but I wrote it one day when I felt lonely and then had a good cry afterwards. I never thought it would go where it could tell tales.

MR. B. I read that, I think "Perhaps she would find comfort in my love", and I come. But it is not easy, because, although everyone makes me welcome, I could not find it in my heart to take you from this so happy home until I could haf prospect of one to gif you. How could I ask you to gif up so much for a poor old fellow who has no fortune but a little learning?

Jo. I'm so glad you are poor; I couldn't bear a rich husband! We have never had wealth as a family, and I have been happy working for those I love—and shall be again. (*She lays a reassuring hand on his.*) And don't call yourself old—I never think of it—I couldn't help loving you if you were seventy!

MR. B. You make me very happy; but haf you patience to wait a long time, Jo? Can you hope and wait while I go away and do my work and save for a home?

Jo. Yes, I know I can; for we love one another and that makes all the rest easy to bear. I have my duty also, and my work. I couldn't enjoy myself if I neglected them even for you—so there's no need of hurry or impatience. You can do your part out West—I can do mine here—and both be happy hoping for the best, and leaving the future to be as God wills.

MR. B. Ah! Thou givest me such hope and courage, and I haf nothing to give back but a full heart and these empty hands.

　　　(*He holds his hands out gently towards her.* Jo *smiles lovingly at him, and with equal gentleness lays her hands in his.*)

Jo. Not empty now, my dear, not empty now.

　　　They sit looking at each other, without moving as the lights gently fade and

　　　　　　　THE CURTAIN FALLS

```
                    BACKING
  _____

   _____
  |           |
  |  STAIRS   |           ↑
  |_____|
  ↕                   TO FRONT DOOR
  |           |
  |_____|
                                              WINDOW
                      ARCH           CUPBOARD  _____    _____         _____
                      ╎                       |      |  | TABLE|       | CABINET|     _____
                      ╎                       |_____|  |_____|       |_____|    | PIANO |
                      ╎                          _____                          |_____|
                      ╎                         |   TABLE   |                           ▢
                      ╎                         |           |
                      ╎                          _____/     ◇ CHAIR
                      ╎                                         _____
                      ╎                                        |                |
                      ╎                                        |      SOFA      |
                      ╎                                        |_____|
                      ╎
                     ___
                  ARMCHAIR
                  _____
                    OIL
                    LAMP
                    ○ TABLE
                                           FIREPLACE
                                       _____
                                                     | TABLE |
                                                     |_____|
                                                    BOOKS  ARMCHAIR
```

(Stage floor plan diagram — labels: BACKING, STAIRS, TO FRONT DOOR, ARCH, WINDOW, CUPBOARD, TABLE, CABINET, PIANO, CHAIR, SOFA, ARMCHAIR, OIL LAMP, TABLE, FIREPLACE, TABLE, BOOKS, ARMCHAIR)

www.ingramcontent.com/pod-product-compliance
Ingram Content Group UK Ltd.
Pitfield, Milton Keynes, MK11 3LW, UK
UKHW021846210426
5322IPUK00022B/500